BULLYING IS NOT A GAME

A Parents' Survival Guide

BULLYING IS NOT A GAME

A Parents' Survival Guide

Laurie Flasko, CSP
Julie A. Christiansen, M.A.

Bullying is Not a Game:
A Parents' Survival Guide

ISBN 978-0-9878846-0-2

Published by:

Laurie Flasko & Associates and Leverage U Press

Printed in Canada
First Edition published March 2012

• • •

Table of Contents

Acknowledgements & Dedications

The authors would like to thank:

Erinne Andrews, Therapist; Joan Hyatt, Jericho Counselling; Dee Tyler, Distress Centre; Nadine Wallace, Niagara Regional Police Services; Bonnie Prentice, TALK; Barb Eade, District School Board of Niagara; Jeannie Makund, Way 2 Click; the Project Rewind team, and the John Howard Society for your contributions of insight, helpful strategies, and advice that will help other parents deal with this tough issue.

We also want to show gratitude to Tom Ziglar and his father, the inimitable Zig Ziglar for kindly allowing us to share snippets of Zig's wit and wisdom in our chapter: "Taking Care of the Home Team". Thanks also to Lisa Magaro for patiently working with us to get the cover design just right, and for putting up with our many amendments and changes. You are a talented graphic artist!

We are grateful to all the researchers who have devoted their lives to understanding the complexities of bullying behaviour, from which we gleaned the wealth of strategies and tools for bullying prevention that we have shared with you here. Thanks to Barbara Coloroso for sharing some of her work with us, and special mention to Dr. Debra Pepler who took time out of her busy schedule to read our manuscript, provide us with tips and advice to make it better, and whose foreword graces the first pages of this book.

Laurie wishes to thank:

To my husband and partner Les Flasko who walked with me through the darkness and helped us to survive... I love you!

• • •

My special thanks to Erinne Andrews, Belinda and Melanie, Chris Pierce, Sylvie Gregoire, Rob D'Amario for helping Amanda graduate and for helping me to cope with getting her through school. A special thanks to Julian for supporting Amanda.

What would I do without my family Mom & Dad, Don, Pam, Sarah, Ben, Daniel, Mary, Craig, Hope, Dave, Helen, Nick, Liz and Ti?

Many thanks to my special friends Laura, Mary, Stephanie, Sandra, Julia, Lori, Rev. Schonberg, Joan, Joan, Lisa, Donna, David, Heather, Ed and Kelly. I don't know what I would have done without you. I have shed many tears with you. You have been there for us throughout.

Thank you to Chris Pierce for getting me started on the book and to my amazing friends Trish Heidebrecht, Doug Schonberg and Laurinda Dovey for helping with the editing. You are so generous! I am also grateful to Kathy and Terri for reading the book and supporting me along the journey, and I want to thank Barbara Glanz for coaching me.

And finally to Julie:
Thank you for partnering with me on the book, for helping to tell our story, and for working with me on delivering strategies to help others. I couldn't have done it without you!

Amanda
You are beautiful. I am so proud of you.
Love Mom

Julie wishes to thank:

I want to thank my husband Steve*who has been my best friend and backup ever since we met when I was 15 years old. You are the constant in my life, the common denominator of our home, and your support, patience, and understanding means everything to me. Thanks to my children Cayla, Dylan, and Thomas for being who you are, and for choosing to be people of action who show sensitivity, compassion and fierce support to bullied children. I also want to acknowledge my father, Delroy Grant for being the strong, silent supporter of my work, and for consistently encouraging me to excel in all that I do.

The creation of this work has been a challenging, emotional, and extremely rewarding exercise in research, teamwork, creation, and collaboration. From the bottom of my heart I want to commend Amanda for having the will and the determination to push through the taxing experience and personal aftermath of bullying and for mustering the courage to share her story with the world. Laurie, I thank you for inviting me to take this exceptional journey with you. It has been an honour and a privilege to work alongside you to make your vision a reality.

This book is for the teachers who made me feel safe and special while I was in school: Elizabeth Eagles, Mme. Henri, David Gamble, Rosemary Hoey, and the late Peter Wale... and for my friends, Bill, Tony, and Steve* who did the same when school was out.

Foreword
It Takes a Team with All of Us to Create a World without Bullying

It has been a privilege to read this book, which will be an essential resource not only for parents, but for all those involved in the lives of children and youth who are concerned about bullying. The broad perspectives and advice offered in this book will be particularly important for parents whose children are being victimized or are involved in bullying others. I want to honour Laurie and Amanda for their courage and commitment in telling their tale of struggles as they tried to deal with the damages from persistent bullying. Even though I am often called an "international expert" in bullying, my most important role is as a parent and I too have struggled to keep my children safe from bullying. It is from that perspective that I recognize how important this book is as an encouraging and informed survival guide for parents who are struggling to ensure that their children have positive friendships and are safe in all the places where they live, learn, and play.

Through over 20 years of research, my colleague Wendy Craig and I have come to understand bullying as a relationship problem in which an individual uses power and aggression to control and distress another. If bullying is a relationship problem, then it requires relationship solutions. Bullying is so significant in a child's life because it undermines children's strong motivation to belong among their peers. During childhood and adolescence, peer relationships affect all aspects of development – intellectual, social, emotional, physical, behavioural, and moral. When children's family, peer and school relationships are positive, children develop social skills, understanding, and confidence. When these relationships are destructive, as in bullying, children's wellbeing and social-emotional development are compromised. According to the National Scientific Council on the Developing Child, "relationships are the 'active ingredients' of the environment's influence on healthy human development (2004, p. 1)". So it is essential for all of us involved with children and youth to do everything in our power to promote positive relationships for children so they will develop to their fullest potential.

As Amanda's bullying experiences reveal, the core feature of bullying is the power dynamics. Those who bully are learning how to use power and aggression to control and distress another; those who are repeatedly victimized, such as Amanda, become trapped in an abusive relationship that is increasingly difficult to escape. It is often challenging for us as parents or teachers to see the power that children exert over others. We can sometimes see that children acquire power over another through a physical advantage such as size and strength. It is more difficult for us to see that they also gain power through a social advantage such as a dominant social role, higher social status in a peer group, and/or strength in numbers. We may not recognize when children abuse power that reflects the systemic power within our society by undermining the security of marginalized groups (e.g., racial or cultural groups, sexual minorities, economically disadvantaged, or disabled persons).

Finally, it is sometimes difficult to see when children recognize another's vulnerabilities and use that knowledge to cause distress. These vulnerabilities vary widely, but can include physical disabilities, weight problems, learning problems, sexual orientation, and family background. Children's sensitivities to their vulnerabilities vary considerably: what might not bother one child can be devastating to another. It is important, therefore, for us to put ourselves into victimized children's shoes so we can be sensitive to their experiences and their perceptions of being bullied. It is how they experience bullying that matters, even if it doesn't seem to be a big problem in our eyes.

As parents, teachers and other adults in children's lives, we are essential in solving bullying problems – the children cannot do it alone. Because the power dynamics in bullying are repeated, the children who are being victimized lose power over time while the children who are bullying increase in power in their destructive relationship. With these power dynamics, it doesn't make sense for us to tell a child: "Solve the problem yourself!" – if s/he could have solved it, the bullying would have stopped in the first or second instance. Nor does it make sense for us to counsel a child to "get thicker skin". Being abused by one's peers is a most shameful and humiliating experience. When children are bullied, they try everything that they can think of to stop the abuse. If they are not able to stop the bullying, they need someone to disrupt the power imbalance, take the negative power away from the child who is bullying, and protect and empower the child who is being victimized. This "someone" is most often an adult who is responsible for the children, such as a teacher, principal, or coach. When they are supported by adults, other children who witness bullying can also be part of the solution, rather than part of the problem. Our observations on the school playground revealed that when a child has the courage to intervene, bullying stops within 10 seconds 57% of the time (Hawkins, Pepler & Craig, 2003).

Once we recognized bullying as a relationship problem, we were able to clarify a basic principle for interventions: ***Bullying is a relationship problem that requires relationship solutions***.

Children who are victimized require *relationship solutions* to protect them from bullying, reintegrate them into positive peer relationships, and bolster their social skills and coping strategies. In Amanda's case, she needed to be protected and integrated into a caring group of friends – this did not happen for her.

There are substantial differences among victimized children; therefore, our supports for these children must be based on assessments of their individual strengths and weaknesses, as well as the quality of their relationships within and beyond school. First and foremost, all children who are victimized require protection from the abuse they are experiencing at the hands of their peers. Protecting children from abuse is the responsibility of adults in their lives, as mandated by the United Nations Convention on the Rights of the Child (UNCRC, 1989). Some of the difficulties that some victimized children may experience include problems with: social and assertiveness skills, emotional and/or behavioural regulation, and depressive and anxiety problems. Scaffolding or coaching victimized children to address the destructive challenges they face when being bullied can be provided through empirically validated programs[1], as well as through consistent moment-to-moment support from parents, teachers, and peers. For victimized children, it is the combination of supportive scaffolding to promote relationship skills and the essential support from adults and from their peers that enables them to escape the torment of bullying and gain confidence in developing the friendships that they want and need so much. It is the adults' responsibility to set up a system to monitor the victimized child's wellbeing and social experiences to ensure that the bullying has stopped and that they are safe.

---

[1] Public Health Agency Canada has a Canadian Best Practices Portal with a Violence Prevention Stream (http://cbpp-pcpe.phac-aspc.gc.ca). This portal provides easy access to information on evidence-based prevention programs that have been shown to be effective.

• • •

Children who bully require *relationship solutions* to enable them to learn how to form relationships based on positive interactions and attitudes. When children bully, they are learning to use their power aggressively; they are learning to assert their social power in a manner that may be momentarily advantageous to themselves, but destructive to others. The girls who were bullying Amanda needed many critical relationship lessons so that they could learn to use their power positively, rather than negatively. These lessons would enable them to move into non-violent, positive dating and marital relationships and become nurturing mothers – this also did not seem to happen.

There are many types of children who bully: some have problems with impulsive aggressive behavior, hostile attitudes, and low social competence; others are popular, socially skilled, and have a strong understanding of social dynamics in their peer groups. The latter group of students increases in power through bullying (Feris & Felmee, 2011). The interventions for these diverse groups of students will vary as a function of their capacities and difficulties. The common consideration for working with all children who bully is their eagerness for power and the destructive manner in which they are achieving power. One challenge faced by parents and educators trying to help children who bully others is to redirect this motivation for power away from the negative strategies of bullying to positive leadership skills and opportunities. Children who bully require education and support to find positive ways of gaining power and status among peers. To achieve a relationship solution, children who bully their peers need to be provided with educational consequences – interventions that provide a clear message that bullying is unacceptable and may result in lost privileges such as being isolated during lunch time if they cannot be respectful. They need lessons to build awareness, skills, empathy, and insights, and provide positive alternatives to bullying as a means to be recognized and feel valued in the peer group.

It is important to monitor these children's peer interactions long after the bullying problem occurred to ensure that bullying is stopping. Harsh punishment of children who bully teaches them one thing: that those who have the power get to use it aggressively to control and distress others.

Parents can make a difference. We are our children's first, last, and most important advocates. It is our deep need to protect our children that gives us the drive to work tirelessly to ensure that bullying stops. The advice offered in this book to keep advocating in a calm, firm, and persistent way is exactly what is needed. As parents, however, we cannot solve our children's bullying problems alone. It takes everybody to prevent bullying and promote healthy relationships. It is not until we can work together with teachers, principals, school board, personnel, mental health services, the police and whoever else involved that we will be able to stop the destructive power dynamics. In the end, we will need broad-based social and cultural change throughout society's systems to ensure that it is unacceptable for those who have the power to use it to distress and control others.

Since 2005, we have been funded by Canadian government research funding through the Networks of Centres of Excellence to develop the Promoting Relationships and Eliminating Violence Network (PREVNet – please visit www.prevnet.ca for many resources for parents, children, youth, teachers, etc.). These research grants have supported us to bridge move the knowledge developed through research to those who need it most – those involved with children and youth in all the places where they live, learn, play, and work. PREVNet now comprises 58 researchers and their graduate students and 50 national youth serving organizations. PREVNet is working to enhance the practices of all those involved with children and youth so they can support children's healthy development through healthy relationships. We believe that together we can find solutions to the relationship problems that plague those involved in bullying – both those being victimized as well as those doing the bullying.

Within PREVNet, we believe that everyone involved in children's lives plays an important role in promoting healthy development and that four strategies are essential to prevent bullying problems (Pepler et al., 2011). These include: 1. Self awareness on the part of adults involved in the lives of children, which is essential to ensure they are modeling and interacting in ways that promote children's healthy behaviours and relationships. 2. Scaffolding or coaching – children need constant coaching and support from adults as they struggle with the challenges of a socially complex world; 3. Social architecture – adults need to play an active role in organizing children's groupings to promote positive interactions and discourage negative interactions; and 4. Systems change – children do not change unless the environments in which they are growing up change; therefore, it is necessary to sustain improvements in the quality of relationships within all places where children live, learn, and play. Preventing and addressing bullying problems is up to all of us! When we collectively address this challenge in our moment-to-moment interactions and programming, we can create safe, secure, and equitable schools, families, and communities that activity foster healthy relationships and eliminate violence.

At this point, there is significant awareness of bullying problems and the impact they can have on children's lives. Nevertheless, there is still an unacceptably high level of bullying and victimization in Canada (Craig et al., 2009). These rates of bullying problems highlight the need for effective solutions because all the adults involved in the lives of children involved in bullying struggle to understand the complexity of bullying and find positive, effective, educational solutions. With this resource, parents will have an informed roadmap with tools and encouraging guidance to enable them to protect their child from bullying and survive the torment that bullying creates. I want to extend my gratitude to Laurie and Amanda Flasko and Julie Christiansen for the courage and perseverance to write this book and to reach out to important professionals, such as Nadine Wallace and Erinne Andrews for broader knowledge and advice. I also want to thank you, as the reader, for engaging with this survival guide because it will take a team with all of us to create a world without bullying.

Debra Pepler
York University and The Hospital for Sick Children
Scientific Co-Director, Promoting Relationships
and Eliminating Violence Network

References

Craig, W., Harel-Fisch. Y., Fogel-Grinvald, M., Dostaler, S., Hetland, J., Simons-Morton, B. Molcho, M., Gaspar de Mato, M., Overpeck, M., Due, P., Pickett, W., the HBSC Violence & Injuries Prevention Focus Group and the HBSC Bullying Writing Group. (2009). *International Journal of Public Health, 54,* S1–S9.

Hawkins, D.L., Pepler, D., & Craig, W. (2001). Peer interventions in playground bullying. *Social Development, 10,* 512-527.

National Scientific Council on the Developing Child. (2004). *Young children develop in an environment of relationships.* Working Paper No. 1. Retrieved from http://www.developingchild.net

UN Committee on the Rights of the Child (1989). *United Nations Convention on the Rights of the Child.* New York: United Nations.

Introduction

Can you remember back to the days when schoolyard games were the best fun? Jump rope, jacks, marbles, hide-and-seek, tag – those were the days of innocence. Then the games got more competitive, more "us against them"; games like dodge ball and monkey-in-the-middle, and capture the flag are more physical and strategic. Still, the game was about the game – it wasn't about hurting or humiliating one's peers. Suddenly it seems, too many playgrounds have been transformed into battlefields. Consider the case of the 12 year-old boy who died after an 11 year-old girl punched him in the chest during morning recess[i]. What about the teenager who, at the tender age of 17, died after being "dump tackled" by an opponent at a high school rugby match[ii]? Ponder the case of the 8-year-old girl, who was pulled from her school by a frustrated mom – after more than 160 fruitless visits to the principal's office to try to keep her daughter safe[iii].

When did going to school become such a hazardous activity? Despite the "best efforts" of government authorities, legislation such as the Safe Schools Act has failed to effect a reduction in schoolyard bullying; in fact, Canada has one of the worst records globally for the incidents of bullying in our schools[iv].

Laurie: This book was written in response to the suggestions of friends and family members who know how profoundly families can be impacted by bullying behaviour. My husband and I encountered bullying first hand after learning that our daughter was being brutally tormented by her peers in her last year of elementary school.

During the most difficult times my child, my husband, and I were overwhelmed by the questions, 'Why us?' and 'How much more can we take?' That we might ever again experience a day when every thought was not consumed by how to end the ordeal or put our suffering behind us once seemed inconceivable. Now, years later we know that what we experienced will never leave us entirely, but we also have a new perspective on an issue that continues to affect children and families everywhere. We are hoping that sharing the lessons we have learned during our most trying time as a family, can lead to early interventions and lessen the impact that bullying behaviour may have on other families.

We have learned so much! In particular we recognized the value and importance of building trusting relationships with our children so they feel safe telling us about uncomfortable situations. They need to trust that parents will not overreact and make their situation worse. Most importantly, we have come to understand that although bullying behaviour can have life-long, lasting effects for those involved, *it can be stopped.*

When we use the word 'victim' in this book, it is being used to describe children who are victimized by bullying. While we recognize that bullying is not a black and white issue, with labeled players (bullies/victims/bystanders), we do not wish to downplay the seriousness of bullying by glossing over a completely unacceptable set of circumstances with words that skirt the real issues. Dr. Debra Pepler writes, "bullying is first and foremost about power and those who bully are frequently rewarded for their use of power and aggression"[v]. Bullying behaviour victimizes others. It takes a serious physical, emotional, spiritual and (in advanced cases), financial toll on individuals and their families. In its most extreme form, bullying can be life-threatening. Having said all of this, we are also reminded that a child who has been victimized should not be *defined* as a victim. Someone who is bullied is also a survivor; a person of incredible personal strength and resiliency, who is capable of becoming an over comer.

Having discussed our use of the term victim, it seems only fitting that we also explain our use of the term 'bully.' Again, this is not about labelling, or defining a person by his actions. We use the term here out of necessity and for the reasons described above. We strongly advise parents and educators to avoid its use completely when dealing directly with the children alleged to be doing the harassing and their families. Suggesting that a child is a bully is a sure way to put the majority of parents on the defensive and ensure the complete withdrawal of their cooperation.

Children who bully may have a variety of reasons for their behaviour, some of which could be deeply rooted psycho-social problems. Others may just engage in bullying behaviour because it is perceived as part of the childhood experience. While some will bully, experience consequences, and never bully again, others may have more difficulty changing because of deeper psychological issues. Like those who have been victimized, children who bully also need a great deal of compassion and support in order to develop into emotionally healthy and well-adjusted adults. Failing to provide this kind of support can be very costly over a lifetime.

Although the focus of this material is the sort of bullying behaviour that occurs at school, it is important for parents to realize that the same practices can occur at the neighbourhood playground, during community-based or organized sports, extra-curricular activities, or even on a visit to the local shopping mall. Many of the strategies included in this work are geared to a school environment but may be adapted to the church or the community centre - wherever bullying may occur.

If your child is being bullied you may have no idea how to handle the situation or even be aware of what is in store. This book will provide you with ideas of how to deal with the teachers, school authorities, and other professionals. It will share tips that I have used that may be helpful for your child and your family.

You may be reading this because you have run out of ideas and don't know what to do or where to turn. I want to encourage you. Children are resilient and your child is so fortunate that s/he has you as an advocate. Even though you may feel frustrated and scared, and at times will seem as if there is no change, even small, incremental, positive efforts on your part can keep the forward momentum towards creating a safe environment for your child. My prayers go out to you!

Julie: When Laurie first invited me to be a part of this project, I had long forgotten or blocked the memories of my personal experiences with bullying. As a new immigrant to Canada in the mid 70's, my siblings and I were teased relentlessly for our skin colour, our hair, our accents, and anything else that made us different. In our day and age, words like "discrimination", "bullying", and "politically correct" had no place. In retrospect, as I examine the state of bullying in Canada today, I realize that not much has changed, except now we have names for what takes place in the schoolyards, beyond the supervisory eyes of the playground monitors.

There is no way to explain the hurt that can be caused by hushed whispers, or sideways glances, rumours, Facebook groups, conversations on MSN, or malicious silence. Just as pain is not always visible, the strikes and blows that cause pain are often hidden and kept in the shadows. As Laurie shared her story and that of her daughter with me, I wept. Even though I had personally experienced the meanness of my schoolmates caused by ignorance and intolerance, I found it hard to believe that *children* could willfully conspire together to cause such pain and suffering to

● ● ●

21

one of their peers. I was compelled to come on board, and to ensure that their story and the lessons learned from it are told.

Ask yourself why you are reading this book. Is it because you have a youngster ready to embark on his/her school experience and you worry for his safety? Perhaps you have a child who is being bullied at school and you are desperately seeking answers. You might suspect your child is victimizing others, and you want to know how you should respond.

Maybe you are an educator who is at your wits' end, wanting to help preserve the safety of your students, but you're running out of ideas. How do you know what is working? How do you know that the strategies you are implementing are actually in the best interests of the child being victimized?

Perhaps you are a bystander, or the parent of a bystander – one who sees these things happening, but outside of saying "tsk tsk – someone should do something about that..." you have not really invested yourself into helping find a solution.

This book is for you. As you read it, listen to the voices of the anguished parents. See the children who suffer in silence in an attempt to spare their parents, and the parents who deny the culpability of their children. Hear the voices of teachers and professionals who try (some with great success and others with dismal failure) to make a difference, and the bullies, who learned that the inaction of others made them incredibly powerful.

Listen closely. What will you hear? Look closely. Read between the lines. What will you see? You will see that bullying is not a game. It is a serious issue with far reaching, long-term consequences that affect all of us – individuals, families, communities, and society as a whole. These consequences continue to affect the lives of those impacted long after the bullying behaviours actually stop. Not only will you hear the story of the Flasko family, but you will learn from professionals in the field, experts in research of the power and impact of bullying, and educational and psychological researchers who are working to find ways to remedy this challenge.

We are at the tipping point: we can allow this alarming trend of an increase in incivility to continue, or we can step in now and be the lever that tips the scales towards a safer and more civil society. We all have a responsibility to re-define the rules of engagement. Our hope and expectation is that the stories, suggestions, guidelines, and resources shared within these pages will help you and parents just like you to deal effectively with bullying.

Laurie Flasko and Julie Christiansen

1

Bullying: A Mother's Story

My life changed forever during my daughter Amanda's Grade 8 year, when she was bullied by a group of "friends." That fall, my husband and I had noticed some changes in her behaviour, but since my daughter was gifted at masking the truth to cover her deep sadness and fear, we could not uncover at first what she was really keeping from us.

When I noticed that her friends were no longer coming around, I questioned her. She said they were busy with different activities and so was she. It wasn't until early November, when she developed a vague illness that afflicted her severely each morning but eased off at night that I decided to investigate further by contacting her school. They had known there was a problem since September but failed to inform me. The Vice-Principal insisted she was not able to discuss what happened with my daughter because the matter involved other girls and she was concerned about their privacy. I insisted on knowing what happened which is when I learned the whole story.

The year prior, a new girl to the school had been interested in the same boy my daughter liked. Friction started immediately. The new girl became very popular within my daughter's circle of friends and quickly found a way of leaving some girls out. After the summer of Grade 7, she managed to pull together a clique and my daughter was not included. For her entire grade eight year, my daughter was physically and emotionally bullied by all of her former friends in the class.

• • •

While I cannot list in its entirety the scope of bullying and abuse she endured, I can certainly share the highlights. The girls would huddle amongst themselves, make mean comments and refuse to talk to her. During an assembly they pushed her off the bench so she could not sit with them. At another assembly they kicked her and poked her in the back with poppy pins, causing her to not only endure exclusion, but also public humiliation. Worse, the teacher was aware this was going on, and while she told the girls to stop, she never made sure that it did.

The girls told Amanda what clothes she should and should not wear. They told her repeatedly she was ugly and that she had anorexia—consequently my daughter's best friend started to ignore her. If she was walking with someone in the playground, they would run up and grab that person and make them move away from Amanda. They threw pennies at her. The girls would tell my daughter not to talk and if she did speak, they told her that what she had to say was stupid. They hit her with their belts. They started rumours about things Amanda had said or done. They created a website about popular kids and had kids vote on how unpopular Amanda was. It is important to say that while these individual acts of unkindness do not, on their own sound devastating, when accumulated, they can take a terrible toll on the victim. Consider the analogy: "death by a thousand cuts". One small "cut" might not necessarily damage an individual's physical or mental health, but a thousand daily, unending "little" attacks certainly would.

To be fair, the school did try to intervene. The Vice Principal's solution involved calling my daughter and eleven of her former best friends together into an empty classroom without adult supervision, and telling them to resolve the problem. Over the course of an hour and a half the eleven girls yelled, belittled and finally, through consensus, told my daughter they didn't want to be her friend. But since the VP told them they had to be nice to her, they told her she could eat lunch with them. After this horrific episode, the VP asked my daughter whether they had worked things out and, fearing any number of reprisals, she said they did. That was the extent of the school's intervention.

After this failed intervention, my daughter decided she could not go back to school. After learning the full extent of what had happened, I wanted the parents of the other girls called in to help resolve and correct the situation. The principal refused on the grounds that this would cause chaos and only make matters worse. My daughter wanted to change schools and, after much discussion, we agreed. We did not believe that running away makes things better and we were concerned about what lesson changing schools would teach her. But after talking to other professionals, we learned that our daughter had already tried to face circumstances far beyond her control, circumstances that were proving to be entirely destructive to her.

I did try to confront a couple of mothers, but only after we decided to leave the school. Deep down inside, I feared that my daughter had somehow caused this, and I was afraid the other mothers would not believe me. After all, these girls played at my home, they were "good" girls from "good" families. How could this possibly be true? How could any of us possibly believe the story of one child against so many peers?

I learned later that many of the mothers had heard that a social worker was coming in to talk to all the girls in the class about my daughter's situation and were angry because they thought their daughters to be innocent of any involvement. I understand they never learned the truth and their girls were never confronted or reprimanded. The girls learned that their behaviour had stymied the adults in their lives to the point that they were at a loss to intervene. Secondly, they learned that they could get away with something so wrong that every responsible party in their lives would deny that it had even taken place.

In the meantime, my daughter had started at another school in the same city. After three months of making friends and having a great year, her seeming progress dissipated over night. One of my daughter's new friends happened to be a cousin of a former bully. The cousin slandered my daughter to her new group of friends who turned on her immediately. They called her at home, threatening assault and promising to make her life miserable.

The next day at school they would not talk to her. In the days that followed, they put fake blood on her locker, knowing she became sick at the sight of blood. They wrote threatening notes in her notebooks and on their MSN profiles. Her teacher even remarked how shocked she was to see such drastic changes in my daughter and her new friends— it was as though one day they were best friends and the next day, they weren't.

After three days, the school still had not dealt with the incidents. It escalated to name calling, huddling, sneers, exclusion, and hitting. Then it went underground. My husband and I requested a meeting with the youth worker, board consultant, and principal. It seemed to us that the school board personnel minimized the severity of the situation. We were told my daughter needed to become more assertive, that *she* was overly sensitive to the kids' comments and she was causing their reactions. My daughter had to be taken out of the classroom at recess and lunch to help with four-year old students in order to survive the torment.

This is the point at which our lives started to fall apart. My daughter became a nervous wreck. She started to get migraines and was not able to go to school. The school youth worker tried everything she could to get my daughter to go to school. She would even come and help me drag Amanda out of bed in the morning and drive her in to school. She really was a lovely, caring lady but the situation was beyond all of our experience and wisdom. The bottom line is that my daughter should not have been put back into this abusive situation with expectations that she would be able to cope!

Grade 8 graduation was a day Amanda had looked forward to for many years. Even following the litany of mistreatment she had endured, she was still determined to go and get her diploma. Once again, the bullies found a way to destroy this special landmark in my daughter's life. The girls from her former school showed up to taunt her during the graduation ceremony. It is interesting to note that they were not friends with the girls from this new school until the persecution of my daughter became their common bond. As all of our family and friends watched in shock, these girls, who had grown up partly in our home, yelled and cheered for every student, until it came time for my daughter. Then their silence fell over the crowd. Perhaps their psychological badgering was not apparent to others, but it was very real for us. I was speechless. I wanted to pick my daughter up and run out. How dare they? My daughter could not bring herself to attend the dance afterward because the same girls stood in front of the dance hall waiting for her. They remembered that valuable lesson they had learned about being able to bully with impunity when my daughter first disappeared from their school without a word of reproach to them from an authority figure.

Grade 9 meant more fear and apprehension. After her first two weeks of attending school and seeing these girls daily, Amanda became ill. She was in such a bad state that she could not and would not attend school. I would beg, I would yell, I would threaten, I would cry, but nothing could get her out of bed. She

● ● ●

became suicidal. Our whole family suffered as we watched my daughter suffer. If it had not been for my faith and many prayers during this time, I would not have survived.

Depression and desperation had taken over the entire family. We had no idea how to cope, how to survive, or how to heal. We were living "other people's" lives. How do you handle your daughter's tears when a fellow student announces to her high school class that the reason your child is not attending high school is because she is pregnant? How do you look your daughter in the eye and tell her that other kids won't believe that lie? How do you reassure her that when she goes back to school this same cruel behaviour won't continue? How do you tell your child that she is beautiful and worthy of good friends, or that she will be happy again, without the words sounding empty and unconvincing? How do you tell her there is good in the world when she has not experienced it? How do you heal her broken heart?

For the next two years the bullying continued. Three girls continued to harass my daughter on the Internet. We finally called the police, who confronted the three girls involved. One girl's family was supportive while the other two refused to accept any suggestion their daughter could have been involved. Nevertheless, the harassment stopped. My daughter started a brand new high school where she received enormous support from the entire staff including the youth worker, guidance counsellor and wonderful, supportive teachers.

While it would be wonderful to say that when the bullying stopped, the negative effects also went away, but that is not the case. There were lasting effects from this traumatic experience which affected her ability to function normally at school. Fortunately, the school recognized her unique situation and was very flexible working with her to feel safe there. The school allowed her to work independently at times, coordinated home instruction, and made special arrangements for her to write tests and exams.

As a mom I grieved the loss of her childhood. She destroyed many of the photos that documented her birthday parties, dance recitals, first day of school and Halloween parades. She missed her Grade 8 graduation dance. She missed her high school graduation. She missed many firsts that the bullies were able to enjoy; they took those firsts for granted and didn't think twice about the impact of their behaviour on Amanda. Although time has healed much of the pain and I have worked hard to forgive, I still harbor hurts deep in my heart.

My husband and I are surprised at our daughter's resilience. She has learned to conquer one challenge at a time. After many years of not understanding what was happening to her psychologically, she was diagnosed with Post Traumatic Stress Disorder and anxiety as a result of the bullying she endured. She has also suffered many other psychological and physical complications from the heightened stress caused by the trauma. Some of these effects will be discussed later in the book.

Amanda has told me that her experience will stay with her for life even though several years have passed. It has taken much time and healing for her to arrive at the place where she doesn't think about it every day. This experience affected her self-esteem, her relationships, her health, her ability to attend school and school functions, family relationships, employment and so much more. I could not begin to imagine what becomes of children who are even more vulnerable. Her recovery was a difficult road, but she has worked hard with her therapist to heal, rebuild and grow. She is a survivor with incredible strength, optimism and a zest for life. She is now a full time post secondary student, and we look forward to the day that we will see her graduate University and carry on with her life as a strong, confident, independent woman.

2

Reviewing the Play by Play

If We Could Turn Back Time

What if you could speak to Amanda? What might she say? How would she describe what happened to her and the impact it had on her life? In the section that follows, we have that unique opportunity to see the bullying through Amanda's eyes and hear her thoughts on her experiences in her own words.

Bullying! This is a well known phenomenon that has been around for ages. When you hear the word, "bully" you might think of some big tough guy in the cafeteria who threatens to beat you up if you don't give him your lunch money, but no! In the last few years bullying has become a very important issue, both in and out of schools. So many children and adolescents have been faced with this horrible problem.

I was one of them.

Go back in time with me and see for yourself what bullying was like.

I was 12 years old and in the 8th

grade. From the beginning of that year, I was relentlessly bullied by a group of girls who had been my friends since kindergarten. I remember feeling so excited on the morning of my first day of grade 8. I wanted nothing more than to have a great year with my friends. But that was not the way it turned out.

I still don't quite understand what happened or why, but here is what I remember. Out of a group of 11 girls, there was only one that I didn't really get along with. I don't understand how one girl can affect the decisions made by 10 other individuals. The first day of school in my grade 8 year is when it all started. I arrived and my friends told me I was ugly. I was told that I looked like "crap". They said that I needed to learn to do my makeup and hair because it was ugly. When I tried to interact with the girls at recess I was told to shut up, because what I said was stupid and they didn't' want to hear about it. As the days and weeks went on, I had no one. Even my best friend turned her back on me.

This continued for months. On Remembrance Day, we gathered for a school assembly. I remember feeling little pin pricks in my back. To my surprise, it was one of the students poking me in the back with her poppy pin! Then, I was

• • •

33

pushed off the bench in assembly, and everyone laughed. I felt like a social outcast.

The abuse continued and then it began to escalate. At recesses they hit me with their belts. At lunch time I ate alone, and they laughed and talked about me the whole time. I could not even get a bite of food down without wanting to be sick, so I started eating nothing at all. On fieldtrips I was by myself. I wasn't allowed to sit with anyone on the bus. I knew everyone was looking at me and observing my every move to find something else to laugh at and make fun of. They would kick me and hit me whenever they felt like it. I was told that I was not good enough. And, in my own eyes, at the time, I truly wasn't. They say that if you listen to negative things about yourself long enough, you start to believe it. I suppose that is true, because that is what happened to me.

Each time I went and told the teacher, NOTHING happened. I was told I needed to work out my problems. I was also told I was overreacting, and that I needed to gain self-confidence. I was running away. I did not want to go on.

This continued throughout my first term. In the mornings I would not want to get out of bed. I found it easier to sleep my problems away: I couldn't bring myself to face the living hell I was experiencing. I never told my mom anything. I had no friends and no family that I felt that I could go to with my problem at the time, so I kept it to myself. Little did I know that I was slowly withering away from stress, anxiety, depression; and when I look at it now, I likely had some form of eating disorder as well.

When my mom finally did find out, she was furious. Not at me, but at the school for not calling her. For not telling her what was going on in her daughter's life. The school was well aware the entire time. The most they ever did was put me and the 11 girls in a room with no supervision and asked us to try and work it out. All that happened was they yelled at me and blamed me for everything that was happening. It was then that I was told I was not allowed to be their friend anymore. Believe me, I was crushed. After going home and crying the night away to my mom and dad, I decided I could not stay at that school any longer.

After Christmas break, I moved to a new school not too much further away. My first two months at the new school were amazing. I made new friends and overall it took very little time for the old me to come back. But, as I soon came to learn, when something good happens something really bad often follows.

One of the girls at my new school was a cousin of a girl at my old school. She found out from her cousin that I had been the target of bullying at my old school. I'm not sure what was said, but whatever it was - that was all it took. The bullying at my new school started on March 1st. I had been there for almost exactly two months. This time, the bullying was so severe that I was an absolute mess. The students put fake blood on my locker, they threatened to beat the crap out of me, and one girl in particular told me to watch my back because she wanted to kill me. I was left out again. More than that, this time, I was truly afraid for my safety. Many of the same things that had happened before were happening again. And, just like before, everyone seemed powerless to stop it.

When Grade 9 rolled around, I was full of anxiety. I was a shaky, unbalanced, skinny girl, who was slowly withering away to nothing. I went to school the first few days, but the sudden death of my great grandma shook me to the core, and made it almost impossible for me to continue with school. I was seeing an art therapist that I trusted and had an amazing relationship with. She was helping me with the bullying situation, but unfortunately she was going on maternity leave. This meant that I would no longer have anyone to share my problems with. After my great grandma's death, I never went back to school. I was having nightmares. I was extremely anxious. My migraines continued. I was always sad. I felt depressed, and I just wanted to sleep my life away.

My parents of course, were very concerned, so my mom took me to see our family doctor. I'm sure my mom was at her wits' end. None of us knew what to do. After spending the entire afternoon at the doctor's, my mom and the family doctor agreed that I should go on an antidepressant. I strongly opposed this recommendation, but I really didn't have a choice in the matter. They figured that medications would make things better - little did they know that my experience was about to get much, much worse.

It didn't take long for me to change yet again, into another completely different person. After about two weeks of taking the antidepressants, I started to think about suicide, and I spoke openly about these thoughts to my mother. The medicine made me feel high, like I was in a daze all the time. I knew I was a different person, and I was extremely afraid of myself. My mom later told me that she was very scared of me too. For me, the signs of suicide were clear cut and open - I did not want to live anymore. All I wanted was for the pain to end. I wanted to have friends again. This was just the beginning of what seemed like an endless nightmare.

For the next 3 years, I fought a horrible battle with anxiety and depression. I could not even look at these girls. I could not believe the hurt that they caused me. My anxiety was so severe that I could not move my legs to get out of bed. Of course, my absence caused people to talk, and so the girls started a rumor that I was missing school because I was pregnant.

I was confronted many times by the bullies, and on one particular occasion, the girl that said she wanted to kill me took things too far on MSN. I was very shaken up and went into crisis. My mom ended up taking me to emergency where I saw a crisis nurse and we finally decided to call the police on them. Not a lot changed, but for the first time I felt like I had a sense of power.

My mom took me to the walk-in clinic and the nurse practitioner talked to me and asked me direct questions about suicide. She asked me if I had a plan. She called the hospital and told me I must go immediately. In retrospect, I realize that it was good that the nurse called and made me go because otherwise I might never have agreed.

At the hospital, the doctor changed my medicine and talked with me about my feelings of depression and wanting to commit suicide. Every doctor I saw told me it was alright that I wasn't attending school because I was extremely ill. They advised my parents not to pressure me to go. This was a good thing, and proved to be helpful for my entire family.

During this stage in my life, my emotions were very volatile and extreme; little things would make me very upset. I couldn't hide my suicidal feelings from other people - even though I tried. Each time I felt like I was losing control of my suicidal thoughts, I found it helpful to go to the emergency crisis centre at the hospital. It was such a relief to know I could talk to someone there without having to stay. The challenge was that every time I went to the hospital I had to repeat my story and this reliving of the experience just made me more upset. It seemed to be causing more harm than good. My mother started to write down everything that was happening to me so that each time I saw a new doctor, we could just hand them the written story with my medications. This relieved some of that pressure, because it eliminated the need for me to tell my story over and over. Aside from using hospital services, we also called the crisis team at Niagara Child and Youth Services (now Pathstone Mental Health), who provided phone assistance, and assessment services. My mom also had people from our church come to pray and talk with me.

I was on and off about ten different medicines, none of which seemed to be working for me. I had night terrors. I cried all the time. I didn't want to sleep in my own bed. I was extremely defiant. I dyed my hair red. My entire body hurt. I had panic attacks. I just wanted it all to go away. Sometimes my mom would sleep in my bed with me when I was scared. She would talk me through my panic attacks and help me to calm down. I was rarely left alone - someone was always with me.

I wanted to go away on a mission trip and the only way I could go was if I continued to make progress. This was a good motivator for me. I couldn't attend normal school, so I attended a school at the St. Catharines General Hospital (Section 19[2]). This was one of the best

---

[2] Section 19 is a special classroom for students requiring special supports. This service is provided by the District School Board of

decisions that was made on my behalf. It allowed me to learn in a safe environment, and the support system there helped me through one of the roughest times of my life. My meds were monitored by a psychiatrist, and I was able to see a therapist whenever I needed her. She taught me strategies to help me live my life day by day. She also helped me go back out into the public again.

I started to make progress, and then it was decided that I should return to my normal high school. Returning to school caused me to feel ill again. We did not know at the time that I was suffering from Post Traumatic Stress Disorder. Just going into the school would cause an onset of terror. We were all caught off guard when my suicidal thoughts quickly returned. This time, when I went to the hospital, they admitted me. I honestly thought at the time that this was the worst thing that could happen to me, but now I recognize that being admitted to the hospital is a life saving strategy. I immediately started seeing my old art therapist again, and this proved a great way to process the trauma I had (and was still) experiencing. She played an enormous role in my recovery.

For my three remaining years of high

Niagara in partnership with various community organizations.

school, I was mostly home-schooled. The regular high school was very helpful in ensuring I got all my credits and made accommodations for me whenever I actually attended. I had a support team of my guidance counsellor, the youth counsellor, my art therapist from NCYS (Pathstone Mental Health), and my teachers. They met together with me and my parents and we agreed on a plan of action that was frequently adjusted in order to help me succeed.

After several years of seeing a variety of therapists, doctors, and psychiatrists, I was finally diagnosed with Post Traumatic Stress Disorder. This diagnosis and its treatment has helped me to manage my life and to finally heal. I continued to see my amazing art therapist until my 18th birthday.

Getting better had always seemed impossible. I never knew I had the strength inside myself. Everyone around me gave me the tools and support I desperately needed, but in the end I had to push myself to get better. Today I am completely off medications, and attend Brock University full time, and I never miss a day!

I now have strategies to help me cope. I have achieved so much in the last few years. I have learned that nothing is impossible; that fear is over-rated and most of all, to live my life to the fullest. I have learned that in times when you have absolutely no one, God is on your side and He will be your best friend. Even though I don't accept what the bullies have done, I've learned to forgive them. I hope though, that one day they will ask for forgiveness and become better people.

Being bullied has made me a much better, stronger person. In a way, I'm glad I had to go through so much to get where I am today because maybe I wouldn't be as strong or as informed about this issue as I am. Maybe I would have never gotten sick for that matter. And without the experience of bullying and doing what I had to so I could recover, I might not have the friends, or boyfriend, or grades, or the happiness that I have today.

I was once a victim but I will no longer be a victim. To whoever is reading this, if you are being bullied, know there is hope and you are not alone. Like me and so many others, you can pull through. Be strong. Keep seeking help, and know that you are not alone.

In the last 5 years my life has changed completely. I love the life that I am living and I have amazing people that surround me. It has taken a lot of hard work on my part and a lot of help from others but my wounds have healed. I have learned to forgive those who have hurt me, I accept what has happened to me and I am now able to move on with my life. Bullying no longer consumes my every thought like it once did. They no longer effect my decisions in where I go what I wear and how I act. I feel like "me" again.

One of the greatest pieces of advice that was given to me over my years of healing was to remember that I am the one who gets to choose who I want to be friends with. My art therapist helped me realize this. She told me to pick my team wisely. Like a soccer team... The people on my team support me. We all work together and get along. We have values in common and enjoy spending time with each other. When things get tough I know that these people will be there for me always backing me up and I am so lucky to have them.

After suffering from extreme mental illness and post traumatic stress disorder because of my experience with bullying, I decided that I wanted to make it my life's goal to help others and raise awareness around these very serious issues. Mental illness is not something to be ashamed of. It is not something that people should hide. People with mental health problems are just like you and me. They have thoughts and feelings and most people who struggle with mental illness live a regular everyday life. Mental health disorders are common among approximately 2.5 percent of children and close to eight percent of adolescents, these disorders are serious and can pave the way to things like avoidance of life activities and may even lead to suicide if untreated[vi].

There is a high correlation between bullying and different mental health issues such as anxiety, school refusal and depression[vii]. Approximately 4 in 5 children are bullied at some point in school[viii]. These are alarming statistics and should be taken seriously. Children's lives are at risk at this very moment and a lot of us just sit by and brush these issues off as; children trying to gain attention, children being too sensitive or even sometimes over dramatic. I want people to see how severe this is and how important it is to seek help for these children and youth. I want teachers and educational professionals to be given the proper tools and strategies to use when a child in their classroom or school comes to them and tells them they are being bullied by a fellow classmate. Zero tolerance policies are not enough! My hope is that there will come a day when it is not the victim sitting inside the classroom at recess but instead the bully being isolated and punished to recognize and learn from their mistakes. Or even better, I hope that a day will come when we can all live and play together in harmony.

My hope is that this book will empower parents to make the right decisions for their children, so that they can support them and be part of their team. My mom and dad were my biggest supporters; they both continue to support me in everything I do. My mom was the rock in our family over the hard years. She kept me alive and she led me in the right direction. She took me to every single doctor's appointment, school meeting, and counselling session. She stood by my side the entire time. I am forever grateful to her for taking care of our home team.

I have learned that everyone is special and important; each human being has something positive to offer and has a very unique and important purpose on this earth. It took me a long time to realize this and it was hard for me to see that even the girls who bullied me are included in my sentiments.

I am now getting ready to graduate university with my bachelor's degree in Child and Youth studies and I am looking forward to starting my Masters degree in Social Work next fall. Eventually I hope to obtain my PHD and become a psychologist. My dream is to create a safe and positive world for other youth who are experiencing symptoms and suffering with mental health issues and bullying. I want them to know that they are not alone and that there is hope for them too.

Finally to the girls who bullied me: Thank you for helping me work towards the person I one day hope to be. If it wasn't for what I went through, we all may have continued to be friends but I may have been the bully instead of the victim. Thank you for allowing me to comprehend what it feels like to hurt so that I could be mindful not to hurt others. I now have a confidence to stand up for myself and others when I see something that is not right. While I have been to Hell and back I would like you to know that my life is full and I am a very happy person. I have learned a lot from what happened and I hope that maybe somewhere deep down inside each of you, you took a positive life lesson away from it too. You once made me feel like I was worthless and that I would never have another friend, but I no longer feel that way. It has been a very long journey but I have found great friends that have stuck by me through thick and thin. Finally, I have come to realize that no one can take control of my life or hold power over what I do or who I am. God controls my destiny and He stands beside me every day.

Amanda

3

Bullying Basics

What is Bullying?

Bullying is defined as repeated aggression characterized by the intent to inflict harm, in which there is a power differential between the child who is bullying and the child being victimized[ix]. While bullying behaviour is not unique to the classroom or schoolyard, research has noted that most bullying behaviour discontinues as children mature; thus, most bullying behaviour occurs among children of elementary school age[x]. While bullying certainly continues throughout high school, the literature demonstrates that it certainly peaks during the pre-teen years (in children in grade 7 and 8) and for most, declines as they mature throughout their secondary school years. Be that as it may, there is a percentage of the population that will not "grow out" of their bullying tendencies, and will continue their aggressive and hostile behaviours through to adulthood. Bullying is not unique to a particular "type" of child; there is no stereotype for a bully. Thus it is possible that a child may be bullied in one context but engage in bullying behaviour in another.

Examples of bullying behaviour include: noisily dominating or verbally browbeating a victim; belligerent, domineering, intimidating, aggressive, frightening, or terrorizing behaviour. Intimidation, aggression, and domination are not always noisy or openly visible. Veiled threats, secret messages, intense stares, aggressive body language, as well as passive-aggressive behaviours can also victimize others. In more lay terms, bullying is overt or covert hurtful behaviour directed toward a single victim or group of victims over time. It may be carried out by an individual or group of individuals working together.

In her book *The Bully, The Bullied, and The Bystander*, Barbara Coloroso outlines three kinds of bullying behaviour: verbal, physical and relational[xi]. Verbal and physical bullying are fairly well known and easily identified. 'Relational bullying' describes what takes place when aggressors disrupt their targets' social relationships and can be much more difficult to detect.

Amanda:
The first day of my Grade 8 school year is when it all started. I arrived and got called ugly. I got told that I looked like "crap". I needed to learn to do my makeup and hair because it was ugly. At recess I was told to shut up, because what I said was stupid, and they didn't want to hear about it. As the days and weeks went on, I had no one; even my best friend turned her back on me.

On Remembrance Day, I got poppy pins poked in my back. I was pushed off the bench in assembly, at recesses I was hit with belts. At lunch time I ate alone, they laughed and talked about me the whole time.

Often victims will seem to go along with, or seem not to mind their harassment, but this is generally a result of both their powerlessness to stop the bullying and their desire to prevent more severe bullying by asking for help or confronting the bully. Many bullying behaviours do not seem severe in isolation, but for the victim who experiences them in a series of unrelenting attacks, each 'little' episode can be traumatic.

Consider this: Jenny mistakenly uses the pen of another classmate and when she is called a 'thief', she is laughed at by her classmates. This happens repeatedly, and as Jenny tries to ignore her feelings of embarrassment and hurt, the bully senses her discomfort and escalates the name calling. Over the course of time, the effects on Jenny may be quite palpable for her even though they are hidden from the rest of the world.

As an observer of the exchange, the teacher may view it as harmless joking around; however, for Jenny, she hides the shame and sense of being belittled by her peers by attempting to laugh it off. If perhaps Jenny had the strength to tell her teacher that the name-calling is distressing her, she might be advised that they are only teasing, and that she should "grow a thicker skin". In so doing, the teacher would be unintentionally positively reinforcing the behaviour of the bullies, while Jenny would learn that telling an adult will not help her to feel any safer. Furthermore, this denigrating nickname may be used by the entire class to tease the victim or may continuously recur for a prolonged period of time, or the victim may experience the very same situation as simply one more public humiliation in a growing history. Worse yet, in a situation like the one just described, the

> **Amanda**
> At elementary school I felt so excluded in the playground, I often just wanted to disappear. On fieldtrips I was by myself. I wasn't allowed to sit with anyone on the bus. I felt like I was a social outcast.

● ● ●

unchallenged, public exchange between the bully and his victim increases the power differential between the two. The bully becomes more able and more likely to strike again.

Bullies are likely to use a variety of ways to antagonize their victims. Some of their physical aggression can be blatant, such as pushing, pinching, punching, slapping or throwing things at their victims. Physical bullying can also take place in more subtle ways. Some bullies will intimidate their victims by nudging, cutting in front of them, or invading their personal space.

The experts identify various types of bullying, which mirror Barbara Coloroso's definitions. Behaviours that can be observed and easily measured such as physical aggression and/or violence often get the most attention because of the implications it has for the physical safety of those being victimized. Verbal bullying can also garner a fair amount of attention, again because it is observable and measurable. The least amount of attention is placed on relational bullying, although it is the most harmful to the emotional and mental health of those being bullied. Relational bullying could be brushed off as "normative female behaviour"[xii] but can be identified by intentional attempts to interfere with a target's social relationships, to exclude the target from social activities and interaction, by threatening to deny the victim friendship, or by manipulative behaviours such as spreading rumours. These forms of aggression can be identified as relational bullying when it is repeatedly aimed at someone who is not as powerful as the bully or bullies[xiii].

Laurie: From the outside, bullying may actually look like inclusion. Here's an example. Once, Amanda was in the library with a group of girls. One of the girls suggested that they play a little game. The game rules were this: one girl (the bully) would hit all of the kids in the group over the head with a book. But when it came for Amanda's turn, the bully "accidentally" hit her a lot harder — and then gave an apparently sincere apology. **All the girls laughed because they were in on the true nature of the game.**

This type of subtle bullying is virtually impossible to prove after the fact. Any inquiring adult would quickly have it pointed out that everyone in the group was hit and no one else complained; therefore, the children who bully will maintain that the child being victimized must be overly sensitive.

A great deal of relational bullying is also psychological in nature, such as name calling, spreading rumors, lying about the child, leaving hostile messages in books or desks about the victim, or excluding the child socially. Social or relational exclusion can range from huddling away from and whispering about the victim to publicly inviting everyone but her to an event. Rejecting, shunning, ostracizing and manipulating are also common methods for social or relational bullying.

Other bullying behaviour may include destroying personal property and leaving it for the victim to find. Scare tactics such as putting blood on a locker may be used to exploit a victim's individual vulnerability.

Computers have allowed another way to capitalize on both the positive and negative sides of relationships. Email, online messaging, social networking websites, and text messages are ways for potential bullies to harass their victims. Many of these technologies allow bullies anonymity, which leads to them being even more daring and aggressive than they would be in person. For the victim, seeing himself defamed online or receiving a threatening text message is no less distressing than if it had happened face-to-face. Indeed, not knowing the identity of one's tormentors can escalate a victim's terror far beyond what he would feel if confronted with a known antagonist. Not knowing who to trust amongst one's peers makes for a very lonely, isolated existence.

It is imperative that adults spend some time trying to understand the electronic bullying that can occur as a result of today's technology. Because this technology changes so rapidly, it can be very difficult for adults to even begin to understand all the potential ways their children can come to harm.

Parents with children of all ages need to become knowledgeable and computer savvy. Time invested in learning how to use and navigate technology will be well spent.

4

Identifying the Players

Who Bullies?

The word 'bully' may conjure up images of tough kid (typically a boy) lurking at a neighborhood park in order to pounce on more defenseless children. A real bully is much more likely to be a student in your child's classroom, or the kid next door. Bullies look just like everyone else. They could be teachers' pets or the student who is perpetually on a time-out. Some are only part time bullies. In fact, if most of us are honest with ourselves, we would have to acknowledge a time when we have personally played the part.

Having just one term to try to describe the many types of individuals who engage in bullying behaviour presents a challenge. As there are many ways in which bullying behaviours can be carried out, there are several profiles that can describe bullies. Barbara Coloroso[xiv] defines seven different types of bullies.

Some of these profiles may dovetail with traditional concepts of what bullies are like, but others describe bullying types that may not have been recognized even a generation ago. For instance, Coloroso identifies "nice" kids who only bully their victims when they are in a group. When there is strength in numbers, children may behave in a way that they never would individually.

Laurie: Amanda's friends were all "nice" kids. They played at my house. I enjoyed their company. I never would have considered them capable of being so willfully hurtful, but they fit the profile of "nice" bullies perfectly. Children may be star pupils with straight "A"s, top performers in the arts or terrific athletes; but, they might still become involved in bullying behaviour. Academic or athletic ability does not necessarily correlate positively with pro-social activity. This is one reason why our situation became more complicated – these girls were smart, outgoing, and involved in sports. They were "good kids". They never gave teachers, parents, or principals any reason to believe that they could be capable of this behaviour.

The common stereotype about what drives the bully's behaviour is that bullying is done in order to raise the bully's self-esteem. While this certainly applies in some cases, there are many others in which there is nothing perceivably wrong with the bully's self-esteem. These bullies have become quite used to "calling the shots" and continue to bully out of a sense of privilege. Take for instance, the tall, good-looking, neighbourhood jock. He might be very confident and have an inflated sense of self-worth. With charisma and charm, and a way with the girls, he might also be very aggressive and competitive, and have no problem pushing the other kids around in order to get his way.

Other children who bully may have learned from an aggressive parent that aggression is acceptable and even preferable. Under these circumstances, convincing a bully that there is a problem with his/her behaviour may prove incredibly difficult. Sometimes, aggressive behaviour is misinterpreted as being competitive, assertive and having strong leadership abilities. Whereas on a sports team where physical aggression is viewed as a team asset, a child may believe that he can continue to be aggressive on the playground and will therefore expect to be valued and encouraged by parents and adults.

The majority of bullies do not empathize well, so appeals for bullies to consider their victim's feelings usually fall on deaf ears. Most need to be *taught* empathy. They must see empathy modeled explicitly (and positively reinforced), and will only develop empathy over a long period of time. Bullies need to develop an understanding of proper boundaries before they can be respectful of others.

The bully is much more likely to be known to the victim than not. In a disturbing number of cases (as it was with Amanda), particularly among girls, the bullies start out as friends. From an adult point of view, seeing these children as bullies can be very difficult because they can be extremely clever at concealing their behaviour. Bullying has been identified in a classroom context as intimidating or threatening behaviour that occurs in short, often clandestine interactions of communication, which are often concealed from teachers.[xv]

Too much silence surrounds bullying: not only do the bullies plot to avoid detection, but their victims are too afraid to speak up for fear that doing so will increase the bullying. Additionally, in some cases, the authority figures involved may overlook bullying behaviour, because the children involved are the star pupils or top athletes and do not fit the stereotypical profile of a bully. *Perhaps this trend is telling us that the markers that we typically use to identify children who bully are incorrect.*

● ● ●

Laurie: I remember meeting with the officials at my daughter's school and suggesting that we call the parents of the girls who were bullying her in an effort to stop the bullying. Wanting to prevent further escalation, the principal was not in favour of this and expressed that it would not be beneficial to call the parents. As a result of the principal's decision, the other parents never knew what happened; therefore, they could not know if the rumours and inaccurate stories from their own children were simply that, or efforts to cloud the true nature of the incidents. Hiding and avoiding conflict will not solve the problems.

Only by communicating a strong message and concern can we begin to prevent bullying, and solve and heal the hurts that it causes.

How to Tell if Your Child is a Bully

As a parent, it is possible to monitor your own child's behaviour to determine whether or not she may be at-risk of developing bullying characteristics. A Queen's University study identified aggressive tendencies that can manifest as early as **age four** that may prove to be risk factors for developing antisocial behaviours such as bullying[xvi]. Typically, physical bullying decreases beyond age 6, while relational bullying increases from ages 8 – 11. While the trend is for all forms of bullying to decline as children mature, this is not the case for all children.

If bullying continues into a child's high school years, it can be much more difficult to control and resolve, especially if the child has learned that his or her behaviour can continue without consequence. Drs. Craig and Pepler note that "bullying is a warm-up for long-term relationship problems"[xvii]. They note the following evidence for this claim:

> *From early adolescence, new forms of aggression, carried out from a position of power, emerge. With developing cognitive and social skills, children become aware of others' vulnerabilities and of their power relative to others. Bullying then diversifies into more sophisticated forms of verbal, social, electronic, sexually, and racially-based aggression.*
>
> *The lessons of power and aggression learned in playground bullying can transfer to sexual harassment, dating aggression and may extend to workplace harassment, as well as marital, child, and elder abuse.*
>
> *In our own research, we have found that both girls and boys who bully in elementary school are at high risk for being physically aggressive with their boy/girlfriends in high school – clear evidence that bullying is a relationship problem.* (Binoculars on Bullying, 2007)

Understanding why children bully is an important part of recognizing whether your child is at risk of becoming a child who bullies. Many experts conceive of bullying as a problem that could either be one of relationship with one's self or with others. An online article entitled, "Some Reasons Kids Bully" by Full Esteem Ahead,[xviii] includes the following list. Bullies may engage in bullying behaviour:

1. To gain a sense of power, control, or revenge.

2. To win recognition and status from peers (bullies immediately receive attention necessary to establish power and gain status with peers).

3. To compensate for feelings of inadequacy, low self esteem, insecurity or friendlessness.

4. Poor social skills and inability to communicate effectively.

5. Because of authoritarian parenting or poor role modelling from parents and other key authority figures.

6. Because of "group think" – within the dynamics of a group, behaviours can be more severe than if one were acting alone.

7. To cover up learning problems at school.

8. Because of a predisposition to anger, aggression, and impulsive behaviour.

9. Because they are emotionally unstable and operate in socially dysfunctional ways.

10. Because they have strong leadership qualities but no one to lead, their behaviour becomes misdirected.

11. Because they have been bullied by others.

Bullies may be "trying on" a new behaviour or repeating a behaviour that they realize has benefitted them in some way. These children may not fully understand the impact of their actions, and that their unacceptable behaviours are making other children unhappy. Sometimes mild intervention (such as explaining the negative outcomes of bullying) in its early stages may be enough to redirect the behaviour before stronger consequences become necessary.

Because some bullies are by nature far less empathetic than others, they may need interventions by people with a great deal more authority and expertise than most parents have. This might include counsellors, psychologists, police, or school administrators. In all cases, young people must learn about the harmful effects of bullying as well as the empathy and apology necessary in order to make restitution, achieve restoration, or to reach reconciliation with the victim.

5

Clues that Your Child May Be a Victim of Bullying

Any young person can become the victim of bullying or harassment. When trying to imagine what a bullied child may look like, we often have an image of a passive, submissive or vulnerable child. However, even the most confident child with a supportive family and a good number of friends can become vulnerable and victimized. Some children will try to speak up, only to have their concerns brushed aside by parents or other authority figures who do not realize the full dimensions of what these children are trying to express.

An "effective" bully can undermine a victim's social support system and self-esteem, making any young person a potential target. If this is the case, especially when many victims are able to mask their suffering from friends and family, how are parents to know if their child is being bullied?

The following symptoms are common signs that a child is being bullied. A victim may exhibit one, some or all of these tendencies:

1. Changes in socialization patterns: not visiting friends, or friends not visiting the family home. In Amanda's case, she made up elaborate stories as to why her friends were not around. She would explain that she had spoken with them earlier or that they were talking on "MSN". Other excuses included plans for the weekend, too much homework, or that she preferred to spend time with her cousins.

2. A loss of interest in things the child used to excel in and an unwillingness to join activities where she may meet new friends (e.g. swimming class at a community pool with children from different schools).

3. The child is secretive, withdrawn, or uncommunicative; avoids telephone contact with friends, screens calls or insists on taking calls privately, with possible mood changes resulting afterwards.

4. The child complains about feeling hurt or betrayed by friends.

5. The child makes negative comments about friends, undergoes significant mood changes, or becomes argumentative.

6. A drop in academic performance or the child begins missing class; the child may pretend to be ill or lie in order to miss certain school activities, like school dances or assemblies during the day.

7. The child may genuinely become physically ill when faced with going to school or other activities that the bullies might also attend. Nausea, headaches or migraines are also possible symptoms.

8. The child insists that his or her friends are too busy to get together.

9. The child demonstrates destructive behaviour, such as self-harm or demonstrates extreme changes in body weight.

10. A disruption to normal sleep patterns, particularly an inability to sleep at night as a result of anxiety, or nightmares.

11. Lying: victims lie about attending events such as birthday parties, to which (in reality) they have not been invited.

12. Changes in regular activities, particularly avoiding situations in which your child is likely to run into peers: not wanting to go to restaurants, movies, or other activities where s/he may run into the bullies.

13. Avoidance of certain places like washrooms, halls, cafeterias or lunch rooms, or buses/bus shelters.

14. The child is secretive about computer or cell phone use (hides screen or disconnects before you can see what has been written).

15. A preoccupation with dealing with "friend" interactions via the Internet; often appears very serious when interacting with friends through technology (chat, text, etc.).

16. New friendships with children several years younger, particularly 'safe' children, such as cousins or children of family friends.

17. The child seems frightened to walk to and from school, or is afraid to take the bus.

18. The child begins to bully younger brothers and sisters.

19. Thoughts of suicide.

20. Depending on the age,

> *Amanda:*
>
> *At one point, my "friends" set up a website all about me, and enabled it with a poll. All the students were able to go online and cast their vote for me as the most ugly and unpopular girl in the class.*

the child may start to play with dolls again (this is a pattern with some middle-school girls).

If you think that your child may be the victim of bullying or you have a sense that something is wrong, you will want to gather more information before opening the topic for discussion. Certainly you should discuss the situation with anyone who may have information to share and has your child's best interest at heart in order to gain the widest possible perspective on the issue. Raising your concerns with your partner, your child's other parent or another caregiver will be a good start, but contacting the child's school should be the next step.

For high school students, you can contact the attendance office or vice-principal in order to establish whether your child is missing more school than you are aware. Some students are able to cover their absences by intercepting phone calls and letters home and not all high school teachers call home for even their most chronic absentees. Asking the right questions will help get teachers talking about the behaviour they see in class. Is your child working happily in pairs or groups, or does she exile herself to the back corner of the classroom? Does she interact socially with other children during recess or physical education, or does she avoid being around other children whenever possible?

How to Approach the Bullied Child

If you have determined that your child may be experiencing bullying behaviour, it is time to open a dialogue. Bearing in mind that a bullied child is likely to feel a sense of shame and failure, you should take the most sensitive approach. Be prepared to listen. Ask for details and convey your concern. Parents of bullied children should let their children know:

1. Speaking up was the right decision.

2. That you, together as a family, are truly committed to seeing him/her through this difficult time.

3. That you will be with him/her every step of the way and that now is the time to take action.

4. They will be involved in deciding how to resolve the problem.

5. It is okay to feel angry, sad, embarrassed, or whatever feeling is presenting itself.

6. That as parents, you are proud of your child.

7. It is okay to express his/her feelings and vent, and that you will be a good listener .

When parents see or hear their child's pain, it is normal for them to also become very emotional. Active listening can be very difficult; however, it is one of the best things a parent can do to maintain a connection with the child. Here are some tips:

1. Listen to the whole story and get as many details as possible. Use this as an opportunity to allow your child to express feelings. Sometimes just venting will help alleviate some of the emotional upset. Be patient with your child as s/he relates the story.

2. Allow the child to engage in "free recall" of the events that occurred. Once s/he has recounted the events, ask lots of open ended questions that will help you to obtain more details about the bullying incident. Be sure to let the child lead, and only ask questions that provide more information about the topic that the child is focused on.

3. Once your child has told you all of the details, paraphrase and reflect what you heard. This is important for a couple of reasons. First it

ensures you have the correct information and are not missing any details, and it also reinforces that you are really listening.

4. Use empathy. Validate the child's feelings with statements like "I can see you're really upset by this," or comments that show you can see what s/he's been through. Give your child the message that his/her feelings are legitimate. Give lots of praise, "You're so amazing, being able to express yourself this way".

5. Give your child a hug. Some might try and pull away during this time but it demonstrates that you are loving and caring.

A parent's natural instinct is to rush in and attempt to protect children and solve their problems. That is not always possible and does not teach children how to become confident, competent, and resilient. If your child is able, it is preferable to empower him by engaging him in the problem solving and decision making process. Barrelling in with guns blazing to save the day may only result in reinforcing your child's belief that he is too weak to stand up for himself. There are times, however, when it is appropriate and necessary to intervene, such as when the bullying has been occurring for a prolonged period of time, if your child is unable to resolve the situation on his/her own, or your child is clearly suffering from the bullying. Waiting too long to address the issue can be harmful.

Learning that your child is being bullied could be quite a shock, and it is not uncommon for a parent to struggle with trying to wrap one's head around what is happening and what it means. Be aware that there are a number of thoughts that may cross your mind; however, some of them may be unhelpful when you are pondering how to approach your bullied child.

Here are some typical thoughts that could be experienced by a victim's parent along with an explanation of the difficulty with each particular way of thinking.

Common Thought	Reason to not "go down this road"...
"If we ignore the problem, perhaps it will go away."	The bully won't stop until stopped. By ignoring it, the problem only goes away for you, not for your child.
"What did you do to cause this?" OR "My child must be the one that caused this. None of the girls are her friends anymore."	Many times we wonder what our child did to provoke such a reaction. This is unfair, considering that the harm bullies inflict is much greater than any possible triggers that *might* have initiated the bullying.
"You need to be more assertive"	If your child could be more assertive, she would! Even the most confident child can be bullied by someone who knows how to capitalize on vulnerability.
"Fight back. One good punch and they won't hurt you again"	You are teaching your child to be aggressive. Violence does not stop violence. Using violence risks escalating the situation. In some cases fighting back will be interpreted as if your child is actually the bully and caused the other children's abusive response. Furthermore, encouraging violence or aggression may turn your child into a "bully-victim", one who both bullies and is bullied.

"What's wrong with my child?"	Bullying is not about your child, nor is it a reflection on him/her. It is a reflection of the bully's need for power, control or dominance.
"What's wrong with *me* – what does this say about my ability to parent this child?"	What is happening is not about you! How you respond to these events is most important. Getting caught up in thinking, "I raised a wimp" will not help you to help your child.

6

Get Acquainted with the Other Players

Parents of Children Who Bully

Schoolyard pranks are nothing new, nor is tying kids to a flagpole for fun. Consider this case: a little boy who was tied to flagpole by peers laughed along with them as he was given what is identified on the Internet as "a flagpole wedgie". (Just because he laughed with them doesn't mean he enjoyed being strapped to the pole.) After the fact, some children expressed how horrified they were by the prank. As the scope of the discussion broadened, some parents were disgusted by the behaviour of these schoolyard bullies, but other parents thought it was no big deal. "Just kids being kids". "They don't' mean anything by it". "Leave well

> *Amanda:*
> When the police confronted the parents about the horrific things being posted about me online, the parents accused my mom of tampering with the MSN messages to try and make their daughters look guilty. It was easier for them to blame Mom than it was to believe their children could be so horrible.

enough alone". "Don't blow it out of proportion".

This kind of disparity in parental responses to bullying provides keen insight into the challenges that face parents of bullied children. While some parents will take bullying behaviour very seriously, others will just as surely see it as a non-issue. It is good to keep this in mind when approaching parents, because depending on what they have been told by their child or their opinions on bullying in general, you may not get the response you were hoping for.

Ideally, it would be terrific if the parents of the bullied child and the parents of the bully could sit down together with the children, hear both sides, and work things out. The truth is that this is mostly wishful thinking because no parent ever wants to hear or believe bad news, especially when their child is involved. Be cautious when dealing with other parents. Getting them to recognize that a legitimate problem exists can quickly escalate into a "he said—she said" situation which is entirely counterproductive. The best approach may be to let the school approach the parents of the other children involved.

Once other parents have been confronted, you can expect a range of reactions. Some will empathize, but others will blame. You can expect to hear many parents defend their own children. They may throw stones by way of bringing up things that your child has done – in an attempt to deflect the blame. Other parents may tell you straight to your face that your child deserves anything s/he has had to endure. Some parents may say it is your child that is the bully and twist the stories around rather than dealing with all of the issues at hand.

Responses like these demonstrate failure to take ownership of a situation that is destructive to the well being of their children and yours. In this case the best approach is to encourage the school to deal with the

• • •

other family or families. It is important to be aware that your reliance on the school to intervene may be dependent on what the school staff members believe to be true about bullying.

Teachers, Administrators, and Counsellors at Your Child's School

Schools are responsible for creating positive environments that promote learning; in fact for a school to be regarded as effective, it must ensure the safety for all members of its community[xix]. In a word, the school and school authorities are responsible for protecting your child and ensuring they are safe from bullying. The negative impacts of bullying are far reaching, and include low morale among students, the creation of a climate of fear and depression, an increase in physical complaints coupled with a decrease in school attendance and poor grades[xx].

One particular challenge to addressing bullying in schools is the divergent definitions that are applied to bullying. As was stated in the first chapter, there are several types of bullying, ranging from physical aggression to relational bullying, with relational bullying inflicting the most emotional and mental damage on victims. Despite this fact, the observability of the other forms of bullying creates a false perception that physical or verbal aggression is more severe.

In a study of teachers in training in the state of Arizona, the teaching students were invited to review a grouping of bullying scenarios. The students perceived relational bullying as the least harmful form of bullying, and expressed the least empathy for victims of relational bullying[xxi]. A similar study was conducted with school counsellors, and the results were alarmingly similar. After reviewing scenarios involving physical, verbal, and relational bullying, the school counsellors perceived relational bullying as the least severe of the three forms of bullying. In addition, the counsellors demonstrated the least amount of empathy for children who were victims of relational bullying, and they were least likely to intervene in those types of incidents[xxii]. Counsellors who received bullying-specific training perceived relational bullying as more severe, and expressed more empathy for victims of relational bullying[xxiii].

Given the gravity of these research results, it is advisable that as a parent you should take an active role in understanding your school's policies about bullying. Furthermore, it would be helpful to know what kind of training teachers have been given about bullying and how to handle it.

If you are concerned about your child and decide to take action, follow the proper "chain of command". You are your child's best advocate. Remember this as you attempt to work with the school. Stay strong, calm, respectful, and focused. Your child's well-being is the issue. Do not allow side issues to distract you from your main objective.

From the first moment you hear about the bullying you may feel that it is your child who should be on the playground and the bullies who should be sitting out for inappropriate behaviour. Unfortunately, this scenario is not likely to occur. It may seem like it is your child who is the one being punished. However, studies have shown that when the school develops an intervention plan that engages both teachers and the student body, the bullies can effectively be consequenced for their behaviour, and the school overall will see a reduction in bullying behaviours[xxiv]. Continue to advocate for these kinds of changes – but before you can campaign for a school-wide intervention plan, you must first see to the safety needs of your child.

Assuming the bullying involves classmates only, meet with your child's teacher first. This should keep the situation from getting blown out of proportion too quickly. If you do not get the results you are looking for, or the bullying involves students in other classes, or the bullying is severe you will get better results from arranging a meeting with the principal or vice-principal.

Collaborate with the school authorities to help your child through difficult periods of the day when he is most vulnerable including lunch, recess and any unsupervised periods. Ask the school to help develop a plan for your child to help promote self esteem and confidence. Find opportunities during vulnerable times for the child to be helpful and creative. Helping a teacher with a special project during lunch or recess may be a great way for a teacher to connect with your child and possibly become a mentor. For example, Amanda was asked to supervise the four and five-year-old students and to answer the phones at lunch hour – these were attempts to keep her safe.

Stay strong, calm, respectful, and focused. Your child's well-being is the issue: do not allow side issues to distract you from your main objective.

Reporting Bullying to the School

Document everything. The sheer volume and complexity of the issues you are dealing with make it likely that you will forget details. The notes you take will be necessary to share with the teachers and school authorities. In the future your notes may also prove useful for doctors, therapists, police, other school principals, consultants or other helping professionals.

Prepare yourself emotionally prior to reporting to the school. Have a clear goal in mind. Safety is your number one concern. Have your facts, questions, and expectations clearly identified. Practice how you will present your information and how you will deal with your emotions. Be as professional as possible.

Attend the meeting with a positive attitude expecting a win-win resolution. In order to achieve your goals developing alliances is one of your best options. The old saying *"you collect more flies with honey than vinegar"* is a helpful philosophy. Keep your emotions under control. Along with choosing your words carefully, be aware of your tone and your body language. You may be angry with the situation and how things have been dealt with to this point. While it is natural to become frustrated and want to blame or demand change and action, even when justified these responses may create a confrontational and defensive reaction. Contributing to a hostile environment will make it more difficult for you to engage the school in making a commitment to helping your child.

Communicating your feelings, wants, and needs clearly and objectively will be important. Here are a few pointers to help you become a more effective advocate for your child's safety.

- Express your concerns by sticking to the facts.

- Ask open questions. "Please tell me more about that..."

- Ask the school for its perspective on what has been happening. Express your desire for everyone concerned to have as much information as possible so that you can all make good decisions.

- Paraphrase what you hear being said so there are no misunderstandings.

- Document the key points of the meeting, and any actionable steps that have been agreed upon.

- You and your child may need to go home and debrief after the meeting and come back to discuss your reactions or further ideas and suggestions your child has.

While most schools have a "zero tolerance" or Safe Schools policy, this does not guarantee consistency in how bullying is addressed from school to school, and schools are still striving to establish best practices. This means that even the best intentioned professionals may not know how to deal effectively with incidents of bullying. Your child's teacher may have attempted to resolve the issue and have unsuccessfully exhausted all options. Building alliances will be easier when you demonstrate respect, empathy, and reflective listening. Express empathetically what you hear the other person saying. Acknowledge the teacher's feelings and appraisal of the situation from his/her point of view. "I understand your frustration. I know you have tried to handle this situation." Acknowledging the positives and praising the teacher's efforts to date will help open lines of communication.

Laurie: I have learned it is helpful to always give people the benefit of the doubt, and to expect they are doing their best. Teachers are caring people who want the best for your child as well as the entire class. They want the issue to be resolved but may be challenged and frustrated with how to handle it as well. Being able to demonstrate empathy for their position will go a long way.

School personnel may be fearful of confronting the parents of children who bully. Regardless, schools need to inform the parents of the children who are involved. Parents who are not made aware of the problems in the early stages are inevitably shocked and angry when they discover that the school did not inform them before the situation escalated.

Many times the school may already be aware that bullying is taking place; however, they may also feel that they have already taken appropriate measures to resolve it. School authorities are rarely completely knowledgeable about the severity of aggressive and passive-aggressive behaviours in which their students may be engaged.

Ask about anti-bullying initiatives in the school or the board, but be cautious of the term, "zero tolerance". It can be incredibly disheartening to a child to hear that the school has zero tolerance when s/he continues to bear the brunt of bullying behaviour.

Above all else, avoid name calling, blaming, or personal attacks as this will cause defensiveness and jeopardize **your goal**. "The main thing is keeping the main thing the main thing" – in this case, the *main thing* is helping your child to feel safe at school. Never lose sight of that!

Helpful Hint… Coping with Pre-Meeting Jitters

Prior to the meeting, you may find yourself experiencing nervousness, anxiety, or intense emotion, which may make clear communication difficult. This may cause you to be fearful of how you will come across when you present your child's case to the school. Write down your thoughts, your needs, and expectations prior to going in to the school – then, if you become emotional and have difficulty finding your words, you can refer to your notes, or read directly from them.

7

Developing a "Game Plan" with the School

Contrary to popular belief, simply reporting bullying neither solves it nor stops it from escalating. If the bullying is not dealt with immediately and appropriately, your child will not be safe. This is why your role as a parent advocate is so vital. As you work with the school, it is important that once the bullying is brought to light, that a plan is put in place to ensure your child's safety as well as to monitor the behaviours of the bully or bullies. As you prepare for the planning session, here are some things to consider.

1. Create a plan together with your child and be prepared to present these options to the teacher or principal. Be sure that the details of the plan options are written down as you go along. Have your child present to discuss and agree to the plan, and ensure s/he has the opportunity to express concerns. Depending on the age, maturity level, or the comfort level of your child, s/he may wish to take on a much more active role in self-advocacy. However, be aware that it is okay for you to take the lead in discussions if your child is too young to speak for himself, or does not feel confident that he can adequately express his needs. Give your child permission to say no to things that are not in the plan or that he does not feel comfortable with.

2. State the problem – explain effects, needs, expectations, etc. (Explain your story – get the school to share their point of view).

3. Ask the school what they can do to create a safe learning environment for your child. While the school may have some excellent options available, it is still advisable to have talked things through with your child and have come up with some options that s/he is fully comfortable with.

4. Present your plan as you have devised it with your child. Express to the school authorities that you appreciate their efforts, and explain that you and your child have brainstormed some additional strategies that could augment the school's plan. Some of the strategies may overlap, and that's okay – this only means that you and the school are thinking alike.

5. Agree on a plan together and follow through. If there is any part of the proposed plan that you or your child feels uncomfortable with, schedule another meeting and take some time to discuss them further at home.

6. Hold the school accountable for the responsibilities to which they commit in your negotiated plan. There should be some kind of formalized mechanism to monitor the behaviour of the bullies to ensure the bullying has stopped. Remember to identify your child's situation as urgent and important; otherwise, it may get lost or pushed aside as the school administration is always dealing with many different issues at hand.

7. Consider the plan a "living document"; one that is open for amendment (by mutual agreement from all players).

8. Review the plan with the school and your child periodically to ensure it is working. If the plan is not successful, then a new plan should be negotiated. A plan should be put in place, and it should not be changed unless your child has been made aware of and given his/her personal input into any changes.

9. Check in with your child and with the school to ensure that the bullying has stopped. It is important to communicate with both sides to ensure a positive outcome has been reached.

> **Amanda:**
> The school knew what I was going through, but their best attempt to help was to put me in a room with the 11 with no adult supervision and no support. They told us to try and work it out. All the girls did was call me names and blame me for what was happening. It was then that I was told I was not allowed to be their friend anymore. I was crushed.

Sometimes teachers or administrators will try to bring the students together to resolve the situation. If you feel this will be helpful then give your support BUT some conditions must be attached. If at any time your child does not feel comfortable doing this or feels upset or frightened, DO NOT make them participate. This could cause further trauma to them. Remember s/he is not the one that caused the situation and s/he should not be the one that needs to solve it either.

The adult supervision should be provided by a skilled supervisor; preferably someone trusted by you and your child; an objective third party, someone who has been trained in bullying intervention, or a Child and Youth Worker from the school staff. If left alone, the bullies may see this as another opportunity to inflict further harm on the victim.

Meetings that are supervised should provide an individual debrief afterwards. No matter the outcome of the meeting, the child needs to be reassured that s/he is brave and that s/he will continue to receive unconditional support. This kind of feedback would be most impactful coming from the school authorities (e.g., principal, vice principal, teachers). Apologies from the involved parties, having a safe environment in which to express feelings, ongoing positive reinforcement from teachers, and continuous follow up and monitoring will help to heal a sensitive situation.

If at any time your child does not feel comfortable doing this or feels upset or frightened, DO NOT make him/her participate.

Things to include in the plan:

☑ A safe place

A safe place would be defined as someplace the child can go and get help at any time. For example, if your son is out at recess and the children are picking on him, he needs to be allowed to enter the school staff room without fear of punishment from the school. Your child may not feel comfortable being on the playground and this should not be forced. Some teachers may suggest that children will never solve their problems if they don't learn to deal with them, but remember your child was victimized. He may need time away and a plan for resolution of the problem that works at his pace. Some options you may suggest could include cleaning the class room (if there is adult supervision). Helping another teacher to complete a special project like photocopying or helping in the office answering the phone or supervising younger children may all be good options. Find something your child loves to do or is good at, and look for ways that he can engage in this activity during recess, lunch and other vulnerable periods.

☑ A safe person

A safe person may be a child from another grade or a person in authority that agrees to look out for your child. It could be the school bus driver or an older child who also takes the school bus. A teacher apart from the classroom teacher may be a better choice, as the classroom teacher will need to deal with all students including the bullies.

☑ Allow the child the opportunity to refuse any situation in which they feel unsafe

Sometimes teachers try to bring children together to "work it out" and this may be very frightening and re-traumatizing to your child.

☑ How to deal with feelings

○ It is common for children who are bullied to combat feelings of helplessness, anger, sadness, fear, and low self esteem. (My daughter believed she was what the bullies told her. She heard it from them so much, that she began to believe that she was stupid, ugly, and a loser). Giving children strategies to resist that persistent negative programming will help to bolster their self-esteem. Remind your child that the name calling and other aggressive behaviours of the bullies are a reflection of their poor character – not a reflection of your child. Help him/her to develop and use some key phrases of positive self-talk such as this one that author Jack Canfield[xxv] uses, "No matter what you say or do to me, I'm still a worthwhile person."

o Some children may become so angry they want to fight back. It is important to talk about these angry feelings in a non-judgmental way even if you don't necessarily agree with how the child is choosing to respond. By validating your child's feelings, you will build his/her trust, and together, you can problem-solve other ways to address the bullying outside of fighting back, submitting, or crying.

☑ How to build up confidence and self esteem

o Many schools will bring in a speaker or workshop facilitator once per year who will speak to the students about self-esteem. This is a good practice that should be continued; however, consistent messaging to reinforce positive self-esteem will be needed for a child who is bullied. Some schools may not be aware of this need, nor will they be prepared to offer that consistent messaging. Have some examples prepared of what you would like the school to do for your child: perhaps a teacher mentor, or an older "cool" student to be a mentor and friend. As mentioned earlier, find something your child loves to do or a way help others by using their gifts and strengths in a positive, productive way.

> **Amanda:**
> Children who bully need support in understanding the impact of their behaviours and the importance of relating positively to others: they need to find ways of achieving power and status through positive leadership.

☑ Dealing with bullies and bystanders

- ○ Bullies need to be dealt with firmly and immediately. Teaching them to sincerely apologize and to make amends is a skill that may be foreign to them; however, it is so important for future healthy development.

- ○ Bystanders may make the difference between whether bullying continues or stops. Possibly not knowing what to do or how to help their friend or classmate may be confusing and lead to guilt and shame or worse: repeated behaviour. Take time to discuss ways bystanders can help, what the school might ask them to do if they see bullying happening at school or elsewhere. Encourage the school to reinforce bystanders' positive behaviour and share ways that they can mend hurt relationships.

Ask the school how the administration plans to deal with reports of bullying. Many schools and boards have social workers with a variety of programs that teach civility in the classrooms. Advocate for this programming to be introduced in your school.

☑ Methods for the school to contact you if there are any immediate concerns

- Express your expectation that you will be kept informed of any situations that arise and how they are being handled. Provide the schools with numbers and procedures to contact you or your family member.

☑ Other concerns or suggestions

- Recognize that even the best plans may need occasional adjustments if they do not work. If something in the plan is not working as intended, changes should be made immediately, after consultation with you and your child.

Laurie: One mother told me how much of a difference a caring school can make in a child's life... When her son was attending grade 7 he became very self conscious about a skin disease he had developed that caused the pigment of his skin to turn white in patches. He was easily embarrassed and ill at ease especially when the other boys began poking fun at him in the change room before gym class. She finally figured this out when a pattern of repeated illnesses on Tuesday and Thursday mornings emerged... the illness always cleared up mid-morning, and then off to school he would go.

The school's policy mandated that students must not wear gym clothes to school, so she was not sure what the reaction would be when she asked them if her son could attend school in his track clothes on Tuesdays and Thursdays. With the understanding and assistance of a very empathetic and caring class room teacher, common sense prevailed and the school allowed her son an exception. This simple, small act eliminated all of the teasing and name calling; as a result, her son was able to attend class with confidence.

How to Monitor your Plan

- When new bullying incidences occur, follow up with the designated school contact person immediately. Once again, let the school know your expectation to be contacted and how to do so.

- Incidences of bullying must be responded to with immediate action in order for the consequences to be most effective. Addressing some of the kids one day and the rest two days later does not generate maximum consequential impact that the situation demands.

- Contact the people who participated in the creation of the plan (e.g., teacher, principal, school counsellor, etc.). Encourage them to take responsibility for their promises.

- Remember to document your conversations. Back up requests in writing, saving emails and letters.

Laurie: I remember reporting one of the bullying incidents to the principal of Amanda's school. While he was very concerned about what happened, it took two days for him to talk with all the children involved because of administrative meetings that took him out of the school. As a result, the incident was never properly addressed. The time lag between the incident and the follow up also gave the kids a chance to create and solidify their own version of what happened, and it gave them an opportunity to take the bullying underground.

Be sure that the plan includes someone in authority responding immediately to any new reports of bullying behaviour.

If or When the Plan Falls Apart

Despite your best efforts, the plan may not always be executed as you and your child hoped, or those people accountable for things outside of your purview may drop the ball. It is also quite possible that the bullies may find new ways to intimidate or injure your child. It may be possible to call in professional mediators to help effect a resolution to the situation. If you become involved in these types of meetings, once again be prepared. Look for ways to create a climate of healing, empathy, apology, forgiveness and restoration. (See Chapter 10 for an example of such a program in the Niagara Region).

If having followed the proper chain of command, you are not satisfied with the school's response to your concerns, arrange a meeting at the board level. You will get the best results if your tone is one of care and concern for your child as well as the wellbeing of the entire school. You are entirely within reason to expect a solution that will enable your child (as well as all the other students) to feel safe at all times.

Changing Schools and Other Alternatives

If despite your best efforts the situation does not improve, it is time to consider other options. Keeping your child in an unsafe or threatening environment can lead to permanent long-term consequences for your child. Many times as parents we believe that there is only one way to achieve education but today there are a wealth and variety of options available. Some schools and personnel are more liberal and experienced than others, so take time to investigate and consider each option.

Changing Schools

Let your child tell you what s/he needs. Discuss the pros and cons of starting fresh. If your child wants to "stick it out", then stand by the child every step of the way. Although there is still no guarantee that the bullying will end, don't be opposed to changing schools; it may be the best solution. If your child wants to change schools, then allow it. Changing schools is not running away when you consider that it is your child's personal safety that is at risk. Safety does not mean just protecting your child from physical violence; it also means shielding him/her from emotional trauma. It is important to understand that the victim is involved in a situation with which s/he cannot possibly expect to cope alone.

Do some brainstorming with your child about what s/he wants from a new school. Give permission to ask for things even if s/he thinks the idea would be rejected. There are so many options available; ask lots of questions and dig below the surface of what the school offers for support. Perhaps the school does not have creative ways of supporting a student who is bullied – asking a "what if" question might be just the spark required to ignite some creative problem solving that will generate a workable solution for your child. This needs to be included in the plan.

Perform Due Diligence Before Switching Schools

Find out as much as you can about the new school. Talk to the principal and be upfront about your reasons for changing schools. Before making a switch, identify social connections that the bullies may have with the new school. After you have identified those social connections, evaluate them. Are they risky connections? Don't be opposed to the idea of moving your child to a school in a different city or suburb. You must also remember social media is global. With the advances in Internet technology, bullying has the potential to follow your child to his/her new school.

Your child's new school should have some resources available to ensure that your child is making a successful transition. Meet the teachers who will be instructing your child. Most will be quite willing to pick up the phone every week or two and let you know in person how your child is doing.

Schools are also able to provide more freedom and flexibility to students who need help. Things that may help could include: a safe place to go for lunch, a place to check in the morning when they arrive at school, coming into class late once all of the kids are settled to avoid the social hallway or leaving school early. Be sure to include these options in your child's safety plan with the new school. While this may be the best option, your child may not feel confident in general about himself. This can make him more vulnerable for a repeat episode of bullying even in a new school or with a new set of peers. Conscious action and planning will be needed to help your child be successful in a new school environment.

Alternatives to Traditional School

If changing to a different school is unlikely to provide the results your child needs, then you may need to look into alternative schooling. If need be, there are many ways students can get their education.

In severe cases, a bullied child who develops health complications may be able to complete a portion of her studies through a home study teacher, appointed by the board. Doctor's notes may be required to have this option authorized.

It is important to note that school boards will not likely volunteer the option for you to home school your child, as taking the child out of the school system takes money out of the school. If you are interested in pursuing this option, press and advocate for it. You may be able to home school your child or, depending on your family's resources, you may have him work out a program with an independent learning centre.

> **Laurie:** Amanda had a variety of learning plans through the years, which allowed her to continue her education and to eventually graduate from high school. As a mom, I had to deal with my own issues of her not attending school in a "normal" way. Her sporadic attendance could have lead to failure of grade advancement, but

with some creative discussions with the guidance counsellor and teachers, alternative strategies were devised for her to complete her studies.

One semester she felt particularly vulnerable attending school. She was enrolled in a full day co-op, which she was able to attend with perfect attendance! One semester she fell behind and was also suffering from high anxiety (which was later identified as post traumatic stress), and so we home schooled her during this time. This was one of the best experiences for her because the teacher that worked with us gave her one-on-one time that resulted in an improvement in her marks. This teacher's caring attitude also played a big part in raising her self esteem. I am so grateful to him today, as I believe he played a major role in her ability to succeed in university.

Finally, some boards have special school programs connected to a mental health agency where children can receive their schooling while attending a special class with other children who have mental health illnesses. One semester, Amanda was able to attend a special class connected to a children's clinic at our local hospital. It was a safe place where she could go and focus on her studies without having to worry about continued bullying behaviour, or the stigma of being a bullied child. These programs are not usually well advertised and may take a lot of searching to discover; but they are out there, and may be a viable option for helping your child continue his education during this difficult time.

> **Amanda:**
> Sometimes children don't go to school because they just CAN'T. Teachers may feel that they have wasted their time, but know that it isn't personal - sometimes children are just under too much duress. Showing your understanding and support will mean more to that child than you will ever know.

8

"Going Upstairs": Dealing with Professionals

In most sports games, especially at the professional level, when a controversial play is called, the officials will "go upstairs" – that is, they consult with the league officials, or check the instant replay camera so that they can determine what really happened, and if the decisions made on the field were appropriate. Unfortunately, when it comes to bullying, a similar process must take place. If bullying behaviour persists, and efforts to curb it fail "on the field", then it is time to call in the professionals.

We are using the word 'professional' to mean anyone in a position of authority to help your child, or who has expertise relative to the bullying issue. It is quite possible that before parents have finished addressing the many issues that will arise as a result of bullying, they will have spent a great deal of time meeting with teachers, school administrators, board personnel, doctors, psychologists, youth support workers and even police or lawyers.

Just as you would educate yourself about a serious medical condition you had developed prior to consulting with a specialist physician, you will need to educate yourself about bullying. This will make it easier to understand the solutions offered by the various professionals you are consulting, as well as to gauge whether you feel that your child is being supported to the greatest extent possible. Before you head into these meetings, it is important to understand the various responses you can expect to encounter.

The good, the bad, and the ugly ...

Unfortunately, although bullying has been on the social and educational radar for some time, it is still a difficult and complex situation for many to understand. While some professionals will take a claim of bullying seriously the first time, this is not always the case. Sometimes parents are told that their child is overly sensitive and should learn to become more assertive. Some professionals will go as far as to suggest that your child's actions contribute to him being victimized. The bullying may be minimized and parents labelled as overreacting. This is the easiest way for some professionals to solve the problem: by simply refusing to accept that it exists in the first place.

The unacceptability of bullying behaviour necessitates efforts for change that focus on those who are doing the bullying. Unfortunately, because parents, educators, physicians and the police sometimes struggle with how to deal effectively with bullying, efforts to combat the problem can tend to focus on the victim.

The experts you consult may know a great deal about bullying and psychology, but you are the expert on your child. Given that your access to these professionals may be restricted, it is a good idea to go into appointments well-prepared. Organize your facts. Make a list of important questions you want to ask, any concerns or issues you would like brought up and any resolutions you were trying to obtain.

If you are afraid you may not have enough time to address all the important facts of a case, prepare a document with this information ahead of time so it is well thought out and presented. Having your requests

● ● ●

or documentation in writing also leaves a paper trail that you may need to follow later on.

Usually professionals are very busy people with various priorities. It is imperative that you follow up to ensure they have done what they said they would do when they said they would do it.

> **Laurie:** When Amanda finally decided she could not take any more harassment we called the police. The police promised they would contact all of the kids on the same night in order to create maximum impact. Unfortunately, this did not happen because the officer went on vacation. A couple of children were contacted immediately and then a couple more later on. This approach did not have much impact in efforts to stop the bullying; as quickly as one week later, they had begun to victimize her again.

There must be a sense of urgency with any plan. Get the assurance and commitment from those involved, and hold them accountable. This is true for the teacher, principal, police etc. Interventions or plans to address the bullying situation should be coordinated and implemented immediately. A strategic plan should be in place for who, what, where, when, and how follow up will occur in order to ensure maximum impact.

The following section shares vital information on how to navigate the school and school board systems, as well as "inside" information on school policy and what you as a parent can request and expect from your school.

Schools and School Boards

Barb Eade, a Principal at the District School Board of Niagara has contributed an historical perspective of the schools' approach to bullying, along with several insights into how to work with schools for the benefit of your child and the student body at large.

Several years ago, Niagara area schools implemented "Character Schools", an intentional effort to embed positive character development into the instructional day. This was an attempt to address undesirable behaviours that were becoming too common in our school yards and in school hallways and classrooms. The Safe Schools Act was implemented in 2005, and seemed to have absorbed the principles of Character Schools into a larger program. Now, every other year, all schools must participate in a "Safe Schools" survey. Everyone in the school must take part – that includes school staff and students. With the passing of Bill 157 in Ontario, bus drivers, educators, visitors to the school, as well as school staff, administration and students, are all responsible to address bullying behaviour as soon as they witness it.

> **Amanda**
> Schools need hands on interventions by trained personnel who can facilitate practice and role-plays to train students on effective strategies for creating a safe environment for all. Our schools need more supervision, on the playground, at recess, lunch, and in class. It's not too much to ask schools to develop creative solutions for complex problems.

Schools can also now provide progressive discipline to students who engage in bullying behaviour off campus (such as cyber bullying, or waiting until a child has left school property to physically attack him/her). If a bully's behaviour is impacting the culture or atmosphere at the school, his or her behaviour can be subject to progressive discipline.

As part of their daily interaction with students, teachers need to pay close attention to behaviour that could signal a bullying situation and offer help right away. The best way to deal with harassment or bullying is to put a stop to it immediately. This is one of the primary strategies to ensuring that bullying is addressed and resolved quickly and effectively.

The other key to ensuring that bullying behaviour is minimized in the school environment is consistency. A strong, firm, consistent message from students, staff, administrators, visitors, etc., will reinforce the message that bullying behaviour is unacceptable and will not be tolerated or rewarded.

"Imagine students being instructed that they are responsible for their fellow human beings and that it is right and noble to get involved when someone is being hurt. Imagine a student being able to attend school knowing that his or her classmates, whether friend or stranger are there for them if the need should ever arise." – *The Wounded Spirit*[xxvi]

Laurie and Julie: At this point, it seems prudent to share some basic information about bystander behaviour in order to understand that bullying is not just a relationship between bullies and victims. It is too easy to believe that bullies have a great deal of

power; that children who are
bullied have no power; and that
bystanders just don't care. This
assumption is far from the truth.
The school's role in decreasing or
eliminating bullying behaviour
depends on having an
understanding of the social
dynamics of bullying.
Interventions will have to involve
all three parties in order to break
the cycles of behaviour.

The reality is that bullying affects everyone involved. Many bystanders may be drawn into the event themselves. Bystanders are more respectful and friendly to the bully than to the target and usually give more attention to the bully which reinforces the bully's behaviour. They may even report that the victim got what s/he deserved because of feeling pressured to support the bully.

From a social psychology perspective, we can come to understand why bullying can be so pervasive in school cultures, and why other children (the bystanders) may appear to be reluctant to step in and intervene. It is possible that those who are witness to bullying behaviour are influenced by the bystander effect: the greater the number of bystanders – the less likely they are to help. In fact, the fewer the number of bystanders, the more likely it is that they will seek help for someone in need; furthermore, with fewer bystanders, the speed of response to cries for help also increase. Darley and Latane (1968a), the leaders of this research, present two viable reasons for the bystander effect. One is *diffusion of responsibility*, and the other is *the influence of apparently calm bystanders*.

Imagine you are walking down a crowded street, say, in a large urban center such as Toronto, Montreal, or New York City. Suddenly, as you are waiting for a favourable crosswalk signal, another pedestrian falls to the ground and lie there unconscious. It is likely that everyone standing on all four corners of that intersection might be thinking, "someone should do something", but it may take seconds, or even minutes before anyone jumps into action. This phenomenon may be due to what is called, "diffusion of responsibility". It appears that when there is a group of bystanders, the responsibility for helping someone in an emergency is shared or diffused amongst the group. As a result, no single individual feels as compelled to respond as s/he might if s/he were alone. Often in such cases, everyone else may assume that someone else will jump in, and consequently no one does.

This exact scenario occurred on the streets of downtown Toronto. A man, who was somewhat overweight, and in his 40s or 50's unexplainably collapsed on the sidewalk. Several people continued walking on, acting as though nothing had happened. Others stopped to stare. Eventually, after about 15 or 30 seconds, someone stooped to see if the man needed assistance. This type of response is reflective of the second explanation for the bystander effect known as "the influence of apparently calm bystanders". In this case, although everyone around (including the individual who related this story) was concerned about the man, everyone else seemed fairly calm. This apparent calmness cast a shadow of doubt over the concern. Maybe he just tripped – he'll get up soon. Maybe he is familiar to the other people around here and he does this all the time – otherwise, someone would be quicker to help. If no one else is concerned, maybe I shouldn't be either. The challenge is that despite the "appearance" of calm, all the witnesses of this disturbing event may be very troubled by what they saw, and perhaps ridden with guilt because they did not intervene.

Now, here's the kicker. Recent research has further demonstrated that people are more likely to help when the individual in need of help is attractive, looks like the majority of the bystanders (both in terms of physical features, as well as dress), and appears to belong wherever s/he is. So in the above example, had the man who collapsed been a well-dressed, fit businessman, he might have received aid sooner. Sad but true. In a school environment then, if the bullies are sending out consistent messages that the victims of bullying are "different", "other", or "not belonging" to the norm, it will be less likely that bystanders will step in to assist.

Another possible explanation for the power of bullying behaviour comes from another social psychology theory of discrimination and prejudice known as "Us vs. Them". This theory posits that groups may divide into "in groups" and "out groups", where those in the "in groups" create reasons to disdain, put down, or bully those in the "out groups". This applies to bullying in the sense that individuals in groups can tend to ostracize people who are very much like them based on "artificially created differentiators"[xxvii].

Implications of the bystander effect

The bystander effect does have a detrimental impact on witnesses of bullying behaviour. Studies have demonstrated that not only the victims of bullying suffer negative effects. Those who find themselves in the multiple roles of sometimes bully/sometimes victim/sometimes bystander have been found to be more likely to experience suicidal ideation compared to those who are just bystanders, or those not involved in bullying at all. Furthermore, students who self report as being only bystanders are also at an elevated risk for low mood and suicidal ideation compared to those who have no experience with bullying. "The majority of students in this study were involved in bullying

● ● ●

behaviour at school as victims, bullies, bystanders, or a combination of all three. Those with multiple roles (victim, bully, and bystander) were significantly more likely to report having had thoughts of ending their life."[xxviii]

Despite the fact that fairly little research has been done about the effects of bullying beyond bully, victim, and bully-victim, it has been theorized that witnesses of bullying (bystanders) or those who are aware of bullying at school may experience what is called, "co-victimization". In other words, knowing that some of their peers are unsafe extends the feelings of insecurity to the larger student body. This sense of co-victimization may contribute to mental health challenges for all the students involved.

Tips from an Ontario School Board ... The School Perspective[xxix]

Very often, victims of bullying do not seek help from adults because they fear the bully will escalate the behaviour, or take the bullying more underground, which often happens. This means that school counsellors, teachers and administrators should receive special training on how to prevent, identify and put a stop to all forms of bullying behaviour, including those that are not readily visible or identifiable. In the sections that follow, Barb Eade provides vital information for teachers and parents about how to address bullying when it arises.

> **"Having an anti-bullying policy is not enough. The DSBN ensures that all employees participate in anti-bullying and first response training. A whole school approach**

works best incorporating equity and inclusivity, safety, mental health, and well-being strategies. Establishing a restorative community within classrooms and schools is seeing positive results capitalizing on teachable moments." Barb Eade, Principal, District School Board of Niagara

Debra Pepler states, "Astute, proactive teachers on the front lines offer the best hope to children suffering at the hands of a bully. Teachers need to move quickly in order to ensure that they put an end to bullying before it escalates or causes lasting harm. Schools, parents and communities need to find ways to support teachers who may identify bullying but not necessarily have all the resources to end it on their own."[xxx]

Dr. Dan Olweus says, "It is a fundamental democratic right for a child to feel safe in school and be spared the oppression and repeated humiliation implied in bullying."[xxxi] A caring school can respond to the rights of the child by:

- ☑ Creating a school vision that promotes a climate of equity, respect, caring and tolerance;
- ☑ Establishing and communicating clear rules and procedures against bullying, involving staff, students and parents in the process;
- ☑ Training staff to act as role models, responding sensitively and consistently to bullying situations;

- ☑ Providing adequate supervision in less structured areas;
- ☑ Encouraging reporting of bullying incidents;
- ☑ Developing curriculum and teaching conflict resolution skills that promote communication, friendship and assertiveness skills;
- ☑ Providing consequences for bullying actions.

The Teacher's Role

The teacher is essential to implementing an effective program and consistent response. Teachers can:

- ☑ Commit to the school vision that promotes a climate of equity, respect, caring and tolerance;
- ☑ Be a role model in words and actions at all times;
- ☑ Incorporate expectations for a safe school into the classroom;
- ☑ Participate in staff development opportunities which provides the skills to identify signs, supervise effectively and respond consistently to bullying situations;
- ☑ Develop and integrate social skills programming into curriculum;
- ☑ Maintain adequate supervision in less structured areas;
- ☑ Communicate with parents as to their roles and responsibilities;
- ☑ Listen, observe and respond to situations immediately and consistently;
- ☑ Recognize and celebrate student leadership and commitment to a bully-free school.

A Checklist for Schools

It is useful to know the nature, extent and consequences of bullying in your school in order to raise everyone's awareness of the problem to common level, to motivate everyone to do something to stop the bad things that are happening, and to establish a baseline for subsequent evaluations. A checklist is one easy way to develop and maintain a system of accountability for your school. A suggested checklist is provided for you in Appendix A.

"Playground 101"

An important aspect of bullying prevention efforts should include the active supervision of less-structured areas of the school environment, such as playgrounds, hallways, school buses, and school cafeterias. Once the school needs are established, common goals and consistent expectations of all community members can be implemented. A list of potential situations in which bullying might occur and suggested interventions are provided in Appendix A.

> **Amanda**
> "It was recess and lunch time that I feared the most. There were no safe places, or safe people to go to."

Considerations for administrators include:

- ☑ Assess the supervision needs in the less-structured areas of your school;
- ☑ Provide teachers with clear expectations and guidelines about where, when, who and how bullying is most likely to occur;
- ☑ Give supervisors a means of communicating with the office during unstructured times and activities (e.g., walkie-talkie / cell phone);
- ☑ Maintain an adequate adult-student supervision ratio;
- ☑ Include indoor supervision (e.g., monitor hallway and washroom movement);

☑ Encourage all staff members to spend time on the playground at recess to observe student behaviour in an unstructured setting. This will increase their awareness of common recess problems;

☑ Back up the authority of the playground monitors;

☑ As an administrator, be visible during less-structured times;

☑ Provide training for all school stakeholders, including class room teachers, custodians, playground monitors, volunteers, and office staff.

Develop relationships with your community partners such as the police, John Howard Society, Big Brothers and Big Sisters. Many may have prevention or self esteem programs that can be brought into your school.

Above all it is important to remember rules are there to protect the victim. If the rules fail to protect the victim, then it is time to change the rules! Also be aware that rules and guidelines must be enforced in order to have "teeth". Bear all of this in mind as you review the suggested interventions provided in Appendix A.

The School Perspective on the Parent's Role

Parents are an important key to supporting the students by being actively involved in and supporting school initiatives and expectations. Parents should be aware that schools have expectations of them. Parents can expect that the school authorities should be doing their part to ensure the safety of their child(ren). Parents can:

1. Understand and support school initiatives that promote a climate of equity, respect, caring, and tolerance.

2. Model the school expectations when in the school or participating in school based activities.

3. Watch for signs of distress in children that may indicate a potential bullying situation.

4. Advise children to communicate with staff and ask for assistance when required.

5. Inform the school if bullying is suspected or occurring.

6. Participate as required to respond consistently to bullying situations (ie., interview, case conference, and Student Planner communication).

7. Contribute to the review of expectations and procedures with staff and school council.

For Teachers and School Administrators: Helping the Victims

One of the responsibilities of members of a school community is to do what they can to help victims of bullying. Here are some considerations that may affect how and what help might be given.

1. Teachers, it may be suggested to you that if a person voluntarily comes to you for help, they just want you to listen sympathetically. This type of advice is misleading and may lead to further victimization of the bullied child. Sympathy sounds like this: "Oh you poor thing – how terrible for you!" Rest assured that victims don't want or need your sympathy; as a teacher and a person in a position of authority, victims of bullying need teachers to demonstrate empathy and to take immediate ACTION to help them feel safe.

2. You may also be advised that on occasion the victim may unwittingly provoke others and

bring on the bullying. While this may be the case on very rare occasions, asking questions such as "What did you do?" will only cause the victim to feel as though s/he is to blame for what has happened, and that the bullying behaviour is justified (the victim's fault). In Amanda's case, she was told she needed medications for her anxiety and that she needed to take assertiveness training to make the bullying stop. She already knew how to make good friends, and she had a good group of friends until one child turned them against her. In most cases it is not the victim that needs to learn assertiveness or social skills, it is the bully. It has already been established that some children who bully may lack empathy and other aspects of emotional intelligence. By blaming the victim and suggesting it is s/he that needs social skills development, the victim will feel as though his/her concerns and needs are not valid. You can best help the victim by validating his/her feelings of victimization, and asking questions that are directed at problem solving and creating a safe space for the child.

3. Brainstorm strategies with the bullied child to help him/her cope more effectively. These strategies will be most effective IF the child can rely on those in authority taking action to reduce or eliminate the bullying behaviour.

4. The victim may need specialized help (e.g., youth counsellor, or outside service). It is vital that schools keep the parents informed of any strategies that are being implemented on behalf of their child(ren). Make the parents part of your intervention team, and keep them in the loop. They know their child(ren) better than

you, and may have valuable insights into how best to apply interventions.

5. Intervention on the victim's behalf with the bully or bullies may be necessary. The Legislation requires any adult who witnesses bullying behaviour to intervene immediately. In many cases, it may be necessary to take immediate action without victim involvement or approval. Ensure that the bullied child is safe before walking away from a bullying situation.

6. Keep records of what has been done to help victimized children, and that actions and outcomes are communicated where appropriate, to interested parties, especially to parents.

For Teachers: Helping the Bullies

Bullies need HELP not only because their behaviour is damaging to others, but also because of the harm that they may cause themselves as a consequence of engaging in this type of behaviour. If left unchecked, bullying can persist into adulthood and impact employability, socioeconomic status, future relationships, and even criminality. It is clear that not all children who bully do so for the same reasons. For this reason, bullies may be helped in different ways.

1. **Social Skills:** some individuals engage in bullying because they want someone to do something for them and lack the necessary social skills to acquire what they want. For some students who bully, social skills programs that teach empathy, encourage prosocial behaviour, and non-violent problem solving skills will be useful. See the Appendix B for suggestions of appropriate social skills programming for children who bully.

2. **Co-operative Learning:** often students who bully have little or no experience cooperating with others. Family life sometimes engenders a tendency to bully others, either because family members model such behaviour or because home life is so frustrating that children take their frustration out on others. This information can only be obtained through dialogue with the child who bullies and his/her families.

Opportunities to engage in cooperative learning experiences are important. Social psychology research has found that activities such as working together to solve problems that can only be solved by group cohesion and full participation will decrease feelings of discrimination and hostility and encourage co-operative exchanges and build feelings of friendship.[xxxii] Programs like these are readily available, and some examples are provided in Appendix B.

3. **Consequences:** students who bully sometimes have a strong need to lead or control others. Often, they bully others because they can (in other words, there are no recriminations or sanctions that act as deterrents to their behaviour). Psychiatrist and author, William Glasser says, "There is no such thing as common sense; people do what makes sense to them." People who choose bullying behaviour do so because it makes sense for their immediate goals. The role of teachers and administrators then is to help children who bully to understand that bullying doesn't make sense. This means that bullies must experience the negative consequences of bullying – this may be through the loss of privileges, full suspensions (in which a child is sent home from school), or restrictions from extra-curricular activities. They must also be encouraged to engage in prosocial behaviour with the introduction of positive reinforcements for treating people fairly and respectfully. When this is done effectively, students who have had a reputation for bullying others have

sometimes reformed and taken a leading role in school anti-bullying committees.

4. **Impulse Control:** Where bullying is largely a result of inadequate impulse control, students can sometimes be helped through exercises promoting more thoughtful delayed responses.

5. **Awareness:** Teachers are encouraged to keep abreast of current research about bullying and its impact on the school environment; to be aware of the various forms of bullying (including relational bullying); and to get training specific to dealing with bullying, intervening on behalf of the victim, as well as how to address the behaviours of the child who bullies.

Laurie: I recently heard from a teacher who related a tale of two children who were bullying one of his students who is in a special class. When the teacher witnessed the bullying occurring on the playground, he acted immediately by pulling the two boys aside to address their behavior. Respectfully they were given a choice. The teacher would report them to the principal and call their parents, or they could befriend the boy. The second option entailed playing with the boy for two days during recess and lunch and to make an effort to find out something about him that they didn't know. The boys opted for befriending the bullied child. One boy immediately began to make an effort, but the other did not. The teacher once again called the non-participating boy aside, and reiterated his conditions for not contacting his parents. This boy then decided that he would play with the child as well. The teacher noted that the bullied child was happier and smiling more, and while the three children did not remain playmates, they continued to be friendly. Most important, the bullying stopped. What made the difference for the bullied child was a caring teacher who was consistent in continually monitoring the children and the playground conditions.

What Students Can Do to Help Students

Students are much more likely to go to other students for help than to go to school staff when they are bullied; therefore, students often have a much better and rather more realistic understanding of the nature of the relationships students have with each other. Students are usually around when bullying takes place, especially during school breaks, and when travelling to and from school. Some students are strongly motivated to help resolve interpersonal conflicts and can demonstrate high level skills in mediation and conflict resolution. This means that students can often provide much needed information on bully/victim problems.

Students can participate by:

1. Taking part in the development of the school policy against bullying.

2. Speaking out against bullying at school assemblies and other school functions.

3. Visiting feeder schools to reassure students who will be coming to their school that they can count on being helped if they encounter troublesome students.

4. Helping to publicize bullying prevention policies by designing posters and writing about bullying in school newsletters. Making it known that they will help fellow students who have problems related to bullying (e.g., peer mediation).

5. Giving advice on how they might handle bullying constructively, choose more prosocial solutions to problems, and get help if they need it.

6. Looking out for students who are having problems in their relationships with others and offering them support.

7. Providing staff with information about bullying.

The School Anti-Bullying Committee:

1. Should be composed of students who have volunteered to work together under the leadership of a staff member to help reduce bullying in school.

2. Is ideally represented by students from every grade and with an appropriate gender balance.

3. May include students who have been bullies in the past – provided they have clearly committed themselves to stop engaging in bullying behaviour.

4. Is led by a staff member who provides a sounding board for student ideas on how to counter bullying at school, and who encourages constructive plans and provides the link between student initiatives and school policies.

5. Has a staff member with extensive knowledge of the research around bullying, how it impacts the victims and bystanders, about initiatives that are working in other schools, and the types of bullying – especially the types that are most damaging emotionally to students.

We are grateful to the District School Board of Niagara for sharing their insights with us!

Communicating with Medical Professionals

Another group of professionals that may play a vital role in bullying intervention and recovery for you and your child is emergency and medical personnel. The following section will address strategies for working with emergency and non-emergency medical service providers.

Often, when you call upon emergency services, you may be greeted with different service providers each time. This is especially true if you are brought to a teaching hospital where residents are doing most of the work and the attending physicians are off duty during the overnight shifts. Amanda notes that having to re-tell her story to a new physician each time she visited the emergency department caused her to experience more anxiety and trauma.

Laurie: My solution to this challenge was to type out a detailed explanation of everything that had happened to Amanda thus far, including her first person account in writing, along with a listing of treatments, medications, etc., so that Amanda was spared the repeated trauma of retelling her story. This is something you may wish to do as well. Be sure to include all medications and interventions that have been attempted thus far. Be your child's advocate when talking with medical professionals, but also be respectful and stay in problem-solving mode. More can be accomplished if you do your best to remain calm and maintain an open dialogue with the doctors on hand.

If your child becomes so depressed that she does not want to attend school, medication may be suggested by your family physician. If s/he recommends antidepressants and/or anxiety medication, do as much research about these medications as possible. Go prepared with questions, and discuss with your physician the pros and cons and possible alternatives. Should you decide that medication is an option for your child, make sure a doctor is available to monitor your child, **daily if needed.** Sometimes upon seeing familiar symptoms, doctors may prescribe medications that are not appropriate for your child, and in some cases, could make the child worse. Changes in the child's mood can occur rapidly, and you need to know how to deal with them right away. If your child shows any signs of suicidal thoughts, contact your doctor immediately—this may be due to negative interactions of the medications.

It is also important to remember that hospitals have crisis workers available if your child needs someone to talk to. There are also help lines they can use from home, such as your local Distress Centre. We have included a number of resources at the end of this booklet for your future reference.

Finding a Counsellor or other Support Services for Your Child

Find a therapist that your child **likes** and connects with. After one or two visits your child may already have a sense of whether the counsellor is a good fit. You may also need to try several before settling on one to see him/her through the whole process of healing. Different stages of recovery may require different types of therapy.

It is a good idea to prepare a list of questions that you can have ready for your interview with a therapist or counsellor. Do not assume that because a therapist or counsellor has been referred to you that s/he will automatically be the best fit for your child or your family.

1. What are the counsellor's thoughts or beliefs about bullying?

2. Has the counsellor received training about bullying, the various forms of bullying, and the effects of bullying?

3. Does the counsellor have a good understanding of the short and long term impact of relational bullying for the victim?

4. What is the counsellor's preferred model for providing therapy? Every counselling model has

its own theoretical mindset or philosophy, which may or may not be a good fit for the needs of your child. For example, there are therapists who specialize in Solution-focused Therapy; others use Cognitive-Behavioural therapy, Reality therapy, traditional Psychotherapy, Art therapy, or Narrative therapy. Marriage and family therapists often operate from a different mindset, and even social workers do not approach counselling from the same perspective as a clinical psychologist might. See Appendix B for explanations of each of these counselling models.

5. How will the counsellor work with your child?

6. How will s/he know that the therapy is working? What are the expected or anticipated outcomes?

7. What kinds of strategies or techniques will s/he use to help the child recover?

8. How involved will the therapist allow the parents/siblings to be in the process? Will s/he confer with the parents and provide tips for the parents to help the child at home? Will the therapist be open to talking with siblings and helping them to develop ways of coping and supporting their bullied sibling?

9. Will the therapist work with the family and the school as part of a team to ensure that the best interests of the child are taken care of?

A Counsellor's Perspective on Going Upstairs

Although this book is written primarily for parents of young people who are being bullied, it is clear that the involvement of other professionals or authorities outside of the family or educational unit is sometimes unavoidable. In this next section, we will hear from Joan Hyatt, M.Ed. Counselling, from Jericho

Counselling, who will share a counsellor's unique perspective on how bullying should be perceived and addressed by all the players.

"Learning from the Past"

Forty years ago when I began my journey in the "Human Services Field", the issue of Domestic Violence did not have a name. We told people who were being abused by their partners to "be nicer", "try harder" and just stay out of the way when anger erupted. We overlooked the pain it caused in families, the emotional cost to those who bore witness and the overwhelming trauma to victims. We have come a long way! Today, we understand that violence comes in many different forms; emotional, sexual, physical and alienation from support systems. Today, we have developed stronger laws and intolerance for such behaviour. Programs exist for abusers and supports are available for victims.

Bullying is violence. It also comes in a plethora of forms; it causes tremendous damage to our children, families and our society. Yet with all of the current media about bullying and the emotional and physical costs, still I hear children being told; "don't let it bother you", "you just have to toughen up." As teachers, parents and support providers, we need to realize that this violence needs to be addressed in the same fashion we have learned to deal with domestic violence.

Bullying, like any other form of aggression, is a desire for power, an opportunity to have control and a tool used to make one person feel superior. As a society we have a responsibility to provide support to the victim of bullying and to the individual who is doing the bullying. As we have done for victims of domestic violence we need to provide safe places to talk and feel strong again. We need to assist victims to regain confidence and understand that they are not the problem. Similarly, we need to assist the bully and help him/her find confidence and self-worth without violence.

Parents and teachers may be reluctant to deal with bullying because they are fearful of making a bad situation worse or that they may be seen as overprotective; however, to ignore bullying is to condone the behaviour and to indirectly tell kids who are being bullied that "it is no big deal". Children need assurance and to see evidence that we will deal with bullies.

Police, school officials and care givers need to realize that physical, emotional and cyber bullying of children is a starting place that may lead to escalated levels of violence. Children who bully are more likely to be aggressive as adults. Children who are bullied deal with anxiety and depression that can lead to suicide. We are beginning to see anti-bullying programs in school and there is less tolerance for it in many areas of our society. Still, victims are often silent, fearful that they will be judged or simply ignored.

It is a healthy society that learns from its past and takes the necessary steps to move toward a non-violent future. We have learned to say no to spousal abuse, provided safe environments for individuals to heal and held those who are perpetrators to account; to do less for our children because we accept it as a normal stage of child development is naive and neglectful. Children need to be confident that the adults in their world will deal with bullying and not expect the parties to "work it out". We do not send adults back into abusive environments to "work things out", nor should we expect children to do so.

We have the opportunity to identify children at risk both of bullying and being bullied. We have developed programs to support children in both healing and adjusting behaviours. We have a responsibility to support our schools and judicial system in their efforts to stop such behaviour. We do not ask adults to tolerate violence in the workplace, or in their relationships; to tolerate it for children or young adults is to say we have not learned from our past.

George Santayana (1863-1952) said: "Those who cannot remember the past are condemned to repeat it." Choosing to learn about bullying, to confront it, to insist on accountability for it may mean that it will be unacceptable sooner and our children will live in a society that keeps us all safer. We need to learn from our past......violence is violence and bullying is unacceptable.

Joan Hyatt, M.Ed., Jericho Counselling

9

The Red Flags of Bullying

"Bullying is a warm-up for long-term relationship problems." Dr. Debra Pepler

Up to 25% of students report having been bullied at some point in their lives, and of this percentage, there are a certain number of cases that result in very, very severe outcomes. The consequences of bullying extend from low self-esteem, social withdrawal and isolation, maladjustment on both a social and emotional level, to potential for substance use, and failing grades. Victims may become depressed, experience anxiety, post-traumatic stress disorder, struggle with anger, aggression, or hostility, experience suicidal ideation, or attempt suicide[xxxiii]. The literature also demonstrates that children who are bullied are more likely to experience both mental and physical health difficulties, and that they explore thoughts of suicide more than their non-bullied peers.

We also know that bullying in childhood is a predictor for future behaviours in adulthood. While statistically, bullying behaviour peaks during the senior years of elementary school (age 11-13), some children continue this behaviour throughout high school and into adulthood.

Dr. Debra Pepler, a leader in the study of bullying in Canada states that "bullying is a warm-up for long-term relationship problems"[xxxiv]. She notes that bullying can often peak during the years of transitioning from school to school. As physical bullying decreases during the pre-teen years, relational bullying emerges as a new method of acting out aggression. Pepler notes that "bullying then diversifies into more sophisticated forms of verbal, social, electronic, sexually, and racially-based aggression".

Once a child who bullies has a taste of this kind of power, it may be hard to satisfy his/her appetite for more. If these more sophisticated forms of bullying are allowed to continue without consequence, the child who bullies will learn that s/he can exert his/her power over others in new ways. This may translate into sexual aggression, workplace bullying, mobbing, as well as various forms of domestic abuse. Pepler notes that in her research, bullying presents as a problem of relationship as opposed to one of behaviour − as is demonstrated by the tendency for both boys and girls who bully in elementary school to become aggressive with their girlfriends or boyfriends in high school.

Signs that bullying has gone too far for your child

Research tells us that children and teens are especially vulnerable to trauma, and that the impact of trauma on a child's emotional development can be significant and long-lasting. These repeated traumatic events appear to disrupt the individual's sense of trust in self, others, and the world, leaving him or her to suffer significant helplessness and/or fear. Chronic exposure to bullying appears to increase feelings of distress and has been linked to greater physical, psychological, and emotional symptoms in children.[xxxv] Watch your child's behaviour for signs of **post traumatic stress** or depression.

There may be a Distress Centre or similar service in your geographical area that offers emergency support to people in crisis. Dee Tyler, Executive Director of the Distress Centre of Niagara has generously provided the following information to help you understand better the link between bullying and suicide. The Centre has also offered some suggestions on what to do if you believe bullying has gone too far for your child.

"Bullying and Suicide: Talk about It!"

Cindy is a bullying prevention advocate with Your Life Counts (www.yourlifecounts.org) who lost her 14 year old daughter Dawn-Marie to suicide in November 2000. Understandably, Cindy describes losing Dawn-Marie to suicide as a result of bullying, as the hardest thing with which she has had to cope. Cindy encourages parents to learn more about bullying in order to break the cycle so other children are not hurt.[xxxvi]

Cindy's story is an example of the results of bullying in one of its extreme forms. Having a child that is bullied is devastating. Losing that child to suicide as a result of bullying is life-altering. It is important to learn how to recognize if your child is being bullied. It is equally important to recognize if your child is struggling with thoughts of suicide.

In this section, we will review how to recognize if your child is having thoughts of suicide and what to do if he/she is having thoughts of suicide. The importance of asking directly about suicide will also be reviewed. If you take away one item from this section, let it be the importance of asking about suicide. Going against a long-held myth that *not asking* about suicide is safer, we want you to know **it is okay to ask about suicide**. Actually, *not asking* about suicide is dangerous.

According to the Canadian Mental Health

Association[xxxvii] talking calmly about suicide, without judgment, can bring relief to someone who is feeling isolated. A willingness to listen demonstrates concern while encouraging the person to talk about his/her suicidal feelings. Listening reduces the risk of an attempt.

In 2006 the World Federation for Mental Health (WFMH) reported that "suicide is rarely a spur of the moment decision. In the days and hours before people kill themselves, there are usually clues and warning signs". A person could say such things as *"I can't go on like this"* and *"Nothing matters any more"*. Other common warning signs included the person: becoming depressed or withdrawn; showing a marked change in behaviour, attitudes or appearance; increasing use of drugs or alcohol and suffering a major loss or life change.[xxxviii] The WFMH (2006) compiled a list of warning signs that could help people identify if someone was contemplating suicide:

Situations

- Family history of suicide or violence
- Sexual or physical abuse
- Death of a close friend or family member
- Divorce or separation, ending a relationship
- Failing academic performance
- Job loss, problems at work
- Impending legal action
- Recent imprisonment or upcoming release

Behaviours

- Crying
- Fighting
- Breaking the law
- Impulsiveness
- Self-harm
- Writing about death or suicide
- Previous suicidal behaviour

- Changes in behaviour

Physical Changes

- Lack of energy
- Disturbed sleep patterns (sleeping too much or too little)
- Loss of appetite
- Sudden weight gain or loss
- Increase in minor illnesses
- Change of sexual interest
- Sudden change in appearance
- Lack of interest in appearance

Thoughts or Emotions

- Thoughts of suicide
- Loneliness, lack of support from family and friends
- Rejection, feeling marginalized (feeling like you are unimportant or insignificant)
- Deep sadness or guilt
- Unable to see beyond a narrow focus
- Daydreaming
- Anxiety and stress
- Helplessness
- Loss of self-worth

Youth in BC[xxxix] (http://youthinbc.com/) is an on-line crisis chat service. They support youth in crisis and encourage people to reach out to someone who may be thinking of suicide by saying *"it's okay to talk about suicide"*. Youth in BC uses the acronym W.A.L.K to show people what they can do to help when they are concerned that someone is suicidal.

Warning signs to watch for. Eighty percent of suicidal youth send out warning signs. They are looking for help. Just because you observe the warning signs doesn't mean your child is suicidal. These signs can be an indication that 'something isn't quite right' and it's worth asking about it. Use the above list, from the World Federation of Mental Health, to help you identify warning signs that your child may be experiencing thoughts of suicide.

Ask. This is your opportunity to show that you care, you are worried, and you are concerned about what you have seen. Remember to ask directly. *"Are you having thoughts of suicide?"* or *"Are you thinking about killing yourself?"* Asking these questions will not make your child suicidal. When you express concern for your child, this 'opens the door' for communicating.

It is important to ask directly about suicide because it shows your child that you are willing to talk openly and honestly about his/her thoughts of suicide. In return, it gives your child 'permission' to respond openly and honestly about his/her feelings of suicide. When you give your child 'the go-ahead' to talk openly about his/her feelings you show your child that there is strength in asking for help.

Listen. Believe what your child is saying. Take him/her seriously. Take the time to listen without judging, interrupting or challenging the person. See the section (below) on "Communicating with Your Child about Suicide" for some practical suggestions about how to listen.

Konnect. Do not leave your child alone. Get connected with services in your community that can help. Remember, you can contact a 24-hour crisis line or other services to help you talk with your child about suicide. Services that are available 24 hours are often listed in the front of the telephone book. Many regions offer on-line information services (e.g., 211, community databases, etc.) that will help you connect with 24-hour agencies and other supports in the community (youth counsellors, school counsellors, doctors, mental health professional, spiritual advisor/leader, community health centres, mental health centre, youth crisis services, etc).

It is stressful being a helper to someone who is experiencing thoughts of suicide. Don't do it alone. You can also use services to get support for yourself.

Communicating with Your Child about Suicide[xl] (www.suicideinfo.ca) is a practical, on-line guide that can help you talk openly with your child about suicide. Some suggestions from The Centre for Suicide Prevention (2007) for communicating with your child about suicide include:

Time

- Have the conversation when you will not be interrupted
- Be flexible about the amount of time you will need

Space

- Choose a place with no distractions
- Choose a place that is comfortable and private

Patience

- Before talking with your child, calm yourself and clear your mind of other issues
- Do not interrupt or provide unwanted advice
- Your child will talk about things that are difficult for you to hear. Do not react with anger, shock or frustration.

- Ask questions, one at a time until you have a clear understanding of what your child is saying (even if, at first, things are not apparent or reasonable to you)

Skill

- Start the conversation with "I" statements. *"I heard you say you don't want to be here anymore. I'm concerned and want to talk more about it with you"*.
- Respond in ways that make your child feel heard. *"You seem very upset and confused"* or *"I can see that you are feeling hurt and sad"*.
- Ensure your tone of voice matches your body language. Show your child that you are interested, concerned, and want to help.
- Use open-ended statements to encourage your child to talk. *"Tell me more about..."* or *"I am not sure what you mean about..."*
- Accept and confirm your child's feelings and that his/her problems are important.
- 'Look at the world' from your child's perspective. What you may consider a minor issue may be much more critical to your child.

> **Amanda**
>
> Parents need to be educated about the signs of victimization and appropriate treatment. They need to keep an account of what is happening to their child, advocate for their child when it becomes necessary, and call the police if that becomes advisable. They need to take all threats of suicide seriously.

The Centre for Suicide Prevention reminds parents to think about your child's point of view:

- The stigma of suicide could be a barrier to your child seeking help. Your child may be embarrassed, frightened, or ashamed.
- Your child may look like an adult yet he/she may not have the emotional maturity to explain his/her feelings. Help your child to express himself/herself.
- Your child may not have the life experience or maturity to move beyond the present and cope with what seems like a major life crisis. Your child may not see that the situation could change for the better.

The effects of being bullied are well documented. Youth and children who are victimized experience traumatic and long-lasting effects such as depression, anxiety, low self-esteem, problems in school, and health problems. In extreme cases, bullying can lead to suicide.[xli] Many of the effects of bullying are similar to the 'clues and signals' of suicide. As parents, it is important to recognize these signs and know that it is okay to ask your child about bullying and it is okay to ask your child directly about suicidal thoughts that he/she may be experiencing.

Take the time to listen. Through listening, you will learn/realize/appreciate what your child is trying to cope with. This understanding will help you, to help your child recover and heal from the crisis. Using the support of family, friends, caring individuals, and others (community agencies, services, doctors, etc) will help your child shift from thoughts of "life is not worth living" to thoughts of "things can change and there is hope for life".

Dee Tyler, Executive Director, Distress Centre Niagara

10

The Officials' Perspective on Bullying

"To the world you are one person, but to one person, you may be the world." Anonymous

It has already been established that tackling bullying is a team effort, but sometimes even the teams need a little help. Sometimes a referee needs to make a call. On these occasions it is valuable to know the officials' position on the rules, as well as how the teams should move forward. We are grateful to Nadine Wallace of the Niagara Regional Police Services for contributing this "inside look" at bullying from the police perspective.

"Bullying Problems: The Justice System Needs to Pay Attention"

Why should police worry about bullying? For all kinds of reasons- bullying is a community issue, it's a safety issue and it's a crime prevention issue.

So how do we "tackle" it? Many young people don't know what bullying entails, so the first thing is to make sure everyone understands what we mean when we use the word. Bullying is not teasing; it is not kids learning how to interact: bullying IS intentional cruelty. In order to be truly effective, schools, parents, police, child care centres, sports clubs, everyone working with kids, needs to be part of the process, to work together-MOST importantly we need our kids... we need to talk to them, ask them for their ideas, support them in implementing these ideas and teach them how to speak up safely when they see something they know is hurtful, illegal, or just wrong. When it comes to speaking up and reporting bullying we often ask "We do it, why can't they?" .... But....do we really do it? Do we as adults always speak up?

How many times do we as adults, parents, professionals, let language "slide" that we know is wrong, for example, something we know to be racist or homophobic like the phrase, "that's so gay"? In policing we talk about the blue wall of silence, but every profession, every group of people, has a wall. The truth is there are consequences to speaking up, you may be isolated, and you may become the target of bullying yourself. Someone may lose his /her job. The human rights tribunal or the police may become involved. How do we help each other and our kids speak up despite those consequences? One way is by modeling that courage ourselves.

Bullying is serious and can be criminal. The victimization and the accompanying trauma that kids experience can play a significant role in their development but also in youth crime rates themselves. Not only are kids who engage in bullying at a far higher risk of becoming involved in the justice system, but so are the victims. Studies have consistently found that children who were physically abused were more likely to display aggression in school settings[xlii], to present delinquent and violent behaviours as adolescents[xliii], and to exhibit criminal behaviours as adults.[xliv] It is not kids just being kids and it should not be something that "we all have to go through".

Often police are called to assist in situations involving bullying, factors including trauma, mental health, learning, developmental or addictions issues, may be contributing to a child/ youth's behaviour. We know that ".... early intervention is critical to prevent child delinquency from escalating into chronic criminality given that child delinquents between the ages of 7-12 have a two to threefold greater risk of becoming serious, violent and chronic offenders..."[xlv]

Not only is bullying misunderstood by many adults, but we forget it actually can lead not just to suicide, but to other violence. Some youth who are victimized take matters into their own hands. They may bring a weapon to school for protection, or they may begin to bully others and may become aggressive themselves. A review of school shootings done in the United States after the Columbine massacre found that two thirds of the youth who perpetrated the violence felt bullied and harassed at school.[xlvi]

In the end, whether we see kids as victimized is irrelevant; *it is their perception* that is their reality. If children tell us they feel victimized, we need to find a way to help them feel safe and that is sometimes not easy - developmental and learning issues, mental health, and other issues may impede a child's ability to read situations and faces the way adults do; but we will never address their feelings of safety and of being victimized if we don't start at a place of recognizing where they are coming from.

Youth who are the targets of bullying often have physical or mental health issues, feel isolated, ashamed, sad and lonely - but just suspending or charging a youth who is engaging in bullying may not be enough to stop the problem.

Youth do not respond to police involvement as adults might. The reality of youth brain development means that most youth do not weigh the punishment prior to committing the crime, **although research would suggest they likely weigh the chances of being apprehended**[xlvii]. It is important to note that punitive sanctions alone are found to be associated with increases in recidivism and have no deterrent effect on youth offending.[xlviii] This is just one more reason we need adults and peers working together.

Police and school personnel have unique opportunities to identify these children/youth and to intervene in ways that can address and ultimately change many of the bullying behaviours. Some children/youth may require longer term interventions and/or community supports as well, but these interventions often begin at the school and community level. The child that comes to school and bullies someone may be the same child that had the police at their home the night before because of domestic violence. We cannot address youth crime without also being aware of its antecedents.

If Bullying is Occurring, What Can You Do?

Keep track:

Write things down. Keeping a timeline is invaluable. This can be exhausting, but is very important both to understand what is going on and to be able to develop a plan of intervention.

Ensure the school is aware of your concerns. A ladder approach may be helpful: teacher, principal, Superintendent, Board, or if all else fails, the Ontario College of Teachers. Police may also become involved and there is no right or wrong time to call us. If you feel your or another child's safety is at risk, don't hesitate to call.

Talk to the teacher, principal, police officer about the history of the bullying. It is very important to be as objective as possible, e.g., not to exaggerate or minimize what has happened.

Give as much information as possible:

If your child or the child you are talking about has a uniqueness, whether it be learning, developmental, mental health, try and separate what are working "diagnoses" from actual ones. Many kids become labeled quickly and it is important to have accurate information. Labels are only helpful if they help us understand why a child might be acting in a certain way and how we might support the child in the future.

If a child is using substances, whether legal or illegal, that is important information. Many kids begin using substances as a way to cope and self-medicate. It is important to try and figure out why they are using the drugs they're using.

Cyber safety tips

Space does not equal privacy. Have conversations regularly about netiquette, about what happens when things are posted on the Internet, about how valuable a tool the Internet can be, but that not everything is legitimate and how we have to be critical thinkers when surfing.

Make sure the child/youth is clear as to what the consequences of breaching the "rules" are going to be. If you use parental monitoring software or MSN logging- let them know. This isn't about catching them doing something wrong, it is about teaching them responsibility.

Research has found that rules are important and kids do respect them for the most part. Rules need to be developmentally appropriate and need to make sense. Remember, adolescent brains are a long way from being developed. When they say they don't know what they were thinking, it's probably true: their brain likely left them for a while!

Computers should be in a space that is well trafficked like a kitchen, open concept den area, or a living room - somewhere where you are able to check in easily and ensure things are okay. If a computer is shut down quickly or a program changed, don't hesitate to ask questions.

Kids say things on the Internet that they would never say face to face - it is important to hold them accountable for their language. Threatening, intimidating, defaming someone on-line is usually a criminal offence.

What Might be Helpful when Police Arrive?

If you do call the police, it is important to know that each call will likely result in a report of some kind. Save the "evidence". Capture the bullying with a computer screen shot, by saving the document, and/or by printing it out. You can certainly forward information to yourself, but remember that the properties of the Email or item may change or may not be available at all. The best evidence is the original.

What Can Police Officers Do About Bullying?

- Be pro-active. Have police work with the school youth counsellor or other staff familiar with bullying dynamics and interventions. If doing presentations or interventions, think about how to include parents. Use a youth's strengths, leadership, athletic and academic ability.

- Help youth understand the legal consequences of bullying. Most youth do not understand that their acts may in fact be criminal and what police involvement may lead to.

- Help youth learn how to take responsibility for their actions and to find ways to make amends with the students they may have hurt.

What Can Police Officers do _for_ Youth Who Are Bullied?

- Remind them that no one deserves to be bullied.

- Youth need safe ways to report bullying. Bullied youth usually will not report the abuse; we need them to have a way to tell us what is happening that feels safe for them and engenders trust that we will be able to help rather than make it worse.

- Speak to schools about their policies on bullying and try and work with them to develop intervention plans. All schools have a "zero tolerance" policy on bullying; however, many may struggle with how to intervene. Children/youth often get the message that the policy is not enforced; that there in fact are no consistent consequences. When policies exist, but are not acted upon, the consequences, severity and frequency of bullying is actually far worse.

- Include in the discussion what the victim and the victim's family will be told. Often, victims feel nothing has happened because there has been a lack of communication due to issues of confidentiality; however, it is important for peers to know matters are being addressed in meaningful ways. Bill 212 under the Ontario Education Act has tried to address these concerns.

What Can Police Officers and Other Adults do *with* Youth Who Bully?

- Understand why the bullying is happening - what is at its root. As Drs. Debra Pepler and Wendy Craig have taught us, bullying is a relationship problem, so we need to address it from that perspective. One of the responses that can often be very effective is a restorative justice approach in which everyone has a voice, but the child who engaged in the bullying is supported in understanding how her/his behaviour affected the other child/youth and where the "victim" feels empowered. This process can help youth put themselves in other teens' shoes ... to think about what it must feel like to be picked on, put down or left out.

- Hold bullies accountable by naming the behaviour and explaining the consequences.

- Help youth understand the legal consequences of these acts. Most youth do not understand the criminality of their behaviour, and how police intervention can affect their lives in the future.

- Help youth to find ways to use their power and influence in positive rather than negative ways (e.g., leadership in school, sports team, and/or community service).

- Help them recognize that everyone is unique and different, and that different doesn't mean worse or better.

- Develop a plan that will help these youth recognize bullying as wrong. Help them appreciate the rights of others, and to figure out how to regulate their own emotions and behaviours.

● ● ●

- Include the school and parents in whatever "intervention" is used. Remember this is not a "one stop" problem.

- Encourage youth to talk to someone they trust, like their parents, a friend, a teacher, a counsellor, or coach. Provide them with strategies.

Youth Criminal Justice Act options police can use include:

- Warning

- Caution

- Referral

- Charge

- Extrajudicial sanction

- Court case/trial

A referral is an option police have to refer a youth (with their consent) to a community agency or program that will assist them, or to use Section 19 to set up conferencing circles or in appropriate cases "team meetings". If a youth is being suspended, police could discuss with the school options that help the youth learn while they are serving their suspension.

Many areas now have conflict resolution programs like a youth justice committee that can be utilized, or an under 12 protocol. For services in Ontario, police could check with their local Ministry of Children and Youth Services representative or 211 Ontario. Intervention discussions include talking about any potential mental health issues, about looking into learning difficulties.

In severe cases, youth may be charged and that may be necessary for safety and/or because of the seriousness of what has happened. Our job doesn't end there: just laying charges may not stop the behaviour. The intervention must continue past the police, and include everyone in the life of the child who bullies.

Nadine Wallace, Niagara Regional Police Service

11

Taking Care of the Home Team

"When you have that home court advantage, if you have a mate that you communicate with, love, honor and respect, you will have a balanced life."
Zig Ziglar

Before you can think about helping your child to recover, it is important to understand how s/he may be feeling at the present time. Being a victim of bullying is a very difficult and stressful situation in which to find oneself. Recognize that your child may exhibit a great deal of out-of-character behaviour at home and school.

Children who have been bullied for any length of time may come to feel isolated or that they do not have any friends. It is possible for your child to be very secretive about how s/he is feeling as a result of being bullied. S/he is probably very concerned that your intervention will only make the situation worse. You can also expect a variety of reactions from a bullied child. Some may become very angry and aggressive or withdrawn and passive. It is important then that you be vigilant in observing your child's responses and be ready to assist your child through the various aspects of recovering his/her life.

Helping your child recover

The recovery process will involve helping your child to understand that there are people who *can* be trusted and relied upon. Eventually your child will begin to form new trusting relationships. Things that you can do that may be helpful include:

1. Ask for ways that you can help. "I can see this is really tough. What can I do to support you?"

2. Keep a respectful eye on your child without being too nosy or pushy.

3. Maintain open channels of communication with your child, and demonstrate empathy.

4. Recognize that there will be a limit to how much you can accomplish on your own and consider retaining the services of a professional such as a psychologist or social worker.

5. Beware of becoming consumed with your child's feelings and his/her ability to cope. For example, as soon as your child arrives home, you might immediately start to ask questions about the day. Your intention might be to make sure s/he is okay, but if the day went badly, you might think this is an opportunity to see if your child needs rescuing. Sometimes though, it is better to bite your tongue and just "be there" for your child.

> **Laurie:** As parents we want to know all the details about our child's day: who s/he sat with, who s/he talked to, who s/he ate lunch with, who was nice, who wasn't; and then step in to make it all better. Being this invasive (especially right after your child arrives home from school) may strain communication in your

• • •

relationship. Remember that your child will tell you what s/he wants you to know. Sometimes s/he won't want to talk about today. Perhaps it was so bad, s/he just wants to forget about it for awhile. Or perhaps there is nothing to tell. Applying too much pressure could backfire, and cause your child to shut down and stop communicating with you altogether.

6. Maintain involvement at your child's school and nurture relationships with your child's teacher, principal and parent council.

7. Encourage your child to meet new friends through new activities–outside of existing circle of friends, and outside the city if necessary.

8. Focus all of your efforts on empowering your child: create situations where s/he can make decisions and be successful. Give lots and lots of praise, looking for ways to praise your child every day. Go out of your way to do this. It may be helpful to write a note to yourself to post as a reminder to praise, empower, and be patient, kind and loving even when your child is not.

> **Laurie:** There were days when Amanda was in such a bad mood, I found it hard to remember to praise her. I used to put up sticky notes to remind me to do it. Sometimes I had to reach to find positive feedback, but I would still say, "Thank you for carrying your dishes to the dishwasher..." if that was the most positive thing that

happened all day. Don't say it just once. They will need to hear the same empowering messages over and over for them to believe it.

9. It is important to help develop a child's self-esteem. Try and find activities outside school to do this. Volunteering is one option. Choose an area that the child will enjoy such as walking dogs at the Humane Society or helping out with children at a kids club like Awana, Brownies, or Cubs. Whatever the program, choose something that helps children feel good about themselves. Build on the child's strengths.

   Kids need each other. Find activities that will allow your child to actively participate and interact with other children (e.g., team sports as opposed to tennis or golf. Now, bear in mind that if your child truly loves golf – s/he should be allowed to enjoy that solitary sport as well!). Encourage social interactions to improve self-esteem and confidence as it may be counter-rehabilitative for your child to retreat into computer games or social media. If age appropriate, help your child to find a job where s/he can meet other youth from different schools.

10. Be aware that to leave your child vulnerable to bullying is clearly unsafe but to over protect your child and teach him or her to become a victim will not support their emotional growth.

11. Be cautious that you don't create a situation where a new friend becomes your child's "crutch". Friendship should be a relationship in which both parties have something to share. Your child may begin to feel overly dependent on someone else rather than re-building her own confidence.

12. Laughter can be great therapy. Foster every opportunity to create and generate laughter.

13. Find special times and activities that you can do together like Friday movie nights with pop and chips at home, mini-putt, or "date nights" for coffee with just one parent.

14. Trust your gut. You know your child best. If something doesn't feel right it probably isn't.

15. Art Therapy has been proven to be an effective means for coping with trauma. Ask your child's counsellor if this will be part of the therapeutic process.

16. While it may be difficult to do, monitor your child's use of the computer. If you can keep your child away from Social Media sites do it! However, in the likely event that you will not be able to accomplish this, work out an agreement with your child (like everything else, put it in writing), that outlines the parameters of how the computer will be used. It is also a good idea to have some strategies for what to do if your child experiences cyber-bullying despite your attempts to minimize the risk. Have your child friend you on any social media sites that s/he is on, and that way you can monitor what his/her peers are saying and the tone of their interactions with your child.

17. If someone is harassing your child online, save the message. Print a copy, ensuring that the original time stamp and any other markers that would identify the sender are also saved. Save any harassing comments. Sometimes children may use terms or texting codes that are unfamiliar to you in reference to your child. Be aware of blogs, Social Media postings, Facebook statuses or websites that may target your child. If you find evidence of this type of cyber-

harassment, you want to contact the police depending on the seriousness of its content.

Bear in mind this cautionary tale: NEVER go to a website pretending to be your child. One parent disclosed doing this and revealed that the harm caused was immeasurable. The situation became very complex and the victim's parents were later accused of and charged with bullying the bullies. Limit all written conversation or correspondence with bullies about bullying, as it may be used against you or your child in the future.

18. Don't ignore inappropriate behaviour. Continue to be consistent with all discipline.

As a parent, you may feel frustrated and hopeless. It is extremely difficult watching your child experience bullying and the effects of bullying and not be able to stop it. Understand that these feelings are normal. Watching your child suffer daily without having the ability to step in and stop the bullying could lead you to feel depressed, sad, frightened, angry, and out of control. It is equally true, however, that you will be unable to support your child fully if you do not also nurture yourself. You might find strength in support from a close family member, or a friend who can be that extra-familial support - someone that you can trust and depend on to simply listen.   There are a number of other things you can do to replenish your own strength:

☑ *Utilize your spiritual resources.* The very first item on your list of how to take care of you should involve connecting or reconnecting with your spiritual self. Whatever your beliefs or your faith, studies have shown that prayer, worship, and/or meditation are helpful tools in the rehabilitative process. Incorporating faith-based practices into your daily routine can prove invaluable in helping you to stay focused on the needs of your child rather than falling into cycles of anger and revenge-seeking. Faith will help you forgive more easily – and with forgiveness will come a release of the anxiety, stress, and heightened arousal that accompanies feelings of anger and resentment.

☑ *Guard relationships within the family*, especially between you and your spouse. During these stressful times you and your partner may have different ways of coping, and may have conflicting ideas of how to handle the situation. Invest time in your most valued relationships. The best advice ever given to me was to go for a 15 minute walk together and don't talk about problems for those 15 minutes! The family relationship must continue to be a priority for a variety of reasons, not the least of which is to demonstrate and role model healthy relationships for your child. Letting your personal relationship stress spill over into other areas of the home may negatively impact the overall family relationship. Your child will sense an increase in household stress and quickly equate it to their situation perpetuating the problem. Try your best to avoid heated discussions or arguments about the bullying when your child is present. Above all, do not talk about the situation in front of the child as though s/he is not in the room. If you are going to discuss something that affects your child, include him or her in the conversation. If you are finding that you are unable to manage conflicts that arise, seek professional help by way of a counsellor or a spiritual leader who can help you work through the challenges.

☑ *Watch sibling reactions and interactions*. Make sure bullying does not occur at home. On the one hand, your child may be vulnerable and easily picked on by a sibling. On the other hand, she may be frustrated and take it out on a sibling. This is a good time to find ways to relate to each other as a family.

☑ *Spend time with your family unit.* Do something that is fun giving you a chance to reconnect as a family. Take this time as "bully-free" time – where you all promise to dedicate your emotional and mental energy to the family fun time rather than trying to figure out what to do next. Make a commitment with your family, including the bullied child, that you will not allow the bully's behaviour to permeate every aspect of your family. Play games, watch a movie together, and go out for dinner or for a walk in a park. Do your best to make the bully-free family time a regular occurrence. Plan it into your schedules and get everyone to participate on a weekly or daily basis. Maintaining this kind of routine will help restore a sense of normalcy for your family and for the bullied child and his/her siblings. It will also show the family that being bullied does not have to negatively impact every aspect of your lives as individuals or as a family unit. Finally, family time will help your child to feel safe in a cohesive family unit, which will counteract any feelings of isolation he may experience in his school environment.

☑ *Take what some people say with a grain of salt.* They haven't walked in your shoes.

☑ Allow yourself to feel sad, angry, or frustrated, and express it. You may find that you need to cry. Crying is natural but if it happens too much you may need some professional help. Caution – this is a naturally depressing or sad period. Not all sadness or depression requires medication. It is only one option of many but is often suggested. Make an educated decision before you opt for it. Get through your day–one minute at a time. Keep hold of other "normal" aspects of your life as much as is possible, even when it is difficult.

• • •

☑ Start a *gratitude journal!* (You will need to find things that are positive in your life and think of them often throughout the day). Be thankful for all of your blessings, even if you have to be really creative. Be positive. For example, 'I'm thankful that my child is home tonight and safe.'

Julie: When Anger Affects Your Relationship with Your Partner[xlix]

We know that anger exists, and that it is a basic emotion that is part of the human construct. It doesn't "go away" when we ignore it, and it is an emotion worthy of expressing. If left unchecked and unexpressed, anger can become like a bitter herb that sours the taste of everything you experience. It is like a weed that chokes the joy and excitement out of every experience. It will colour every interaction you have with your spouse - it dilutes trust, and spreads seeds of doubt everywhere - to the point that you can no longer make the distinction between genuine love and feigned affection. So what can we do about this problem? Here are 4 quick tips - ways to keep anger from wrecking your marriage or partnership.

1. Openly discuss how you will communicate with each other when you are feeling angry. Set the parameters for that discussion when you are both calm and level-headed. The physiology of anger puts us in a state that is not conducive to making clear decisions with an eye for future consequences, so it is best to decide on how you will deal with anger BEFORE it occurs. Talk about the kinds of things that might spark anger, and how you can help each other to keep anger-inducing situations to a minimum in the relationship. This is especially important when you are trying to problem-solve around issues arising from your child's experience with bullying. One party may want to rush in guns

blazing, while the other may advocate for a softer approach. While you are both playing for the same team, sometimes you may struggle with agreements on particular strategies.

2. Think before you act. This sounds like a no-brainer piece of advice but it amazes me how many couples take this for granted. For example, imagine what would happen if one parent went off to the school and caused a huge scene because of his/her anger over an unresolved bullying situation. How might the other partner react? Likely with strong emotions and a few choice words about not being consulted – we should have discussed this before you made a decision that affects the whole family – that sort of "conversation". Making decisions that could impact the entire family without discussing it with your partner will undoubtedly result in feelings of resentment that could last long beyond the crisis itself. So take this one seriously - guys and girls alike! Talk to your partner/spouse about what you're thinking. Ask yourself, "What could happen if I do what I want to do?" - "What is the worst thing that could happen? What is the best thing that could happen? Is this worth getting into a fight over?" If you consider the consequences and possible outcomes BEFORE you act, and make an informed decision, your outcomes will always be better.

3. Never play on opposing teams. When you enter into a marriage, partnership, or common-law situation, you are choosing your team. No matter what the issue, whether it is the house, the job, the kids, the dog, the cat, or the hydro bill, you MUST remember that you are playing for and fighting for the same team and you are on the same side. It is rare to see team members

• • •

self-destruct on the baseball diamond or on the hockey rink and start fighting each other. They understand that in order to win, they must play together, and stand up for each other. Marriage and relationships are just like that. When you are fighting about how to raise your kids, remember that these are YOUR kids - you made them together, and you are raising them together. Your end goal is not to mess them up for life; it is to help them become responsible, contributing members of society. You are on the same team. When you look at it this way, it becomes easier to stay *focused on the issue* so that you can solve it together, rather than resorting to **attacking the person** for his/her beliefs or personality flaws. Never lay blame where it doesn't belong. You would be better to take responsibility for your own shortcomings, and trust your partner to do the same for his/hers. Even if you think you are justified in laying blame, go back to point number two: will saying, "It's your fault" make the situation better or worse? It might be better to ask, "Now that we are faced with this problem, what can we do together to fix this?" Work together - play for the same team - fight for the same army. Your marriage and your kids will thank you for it.

4. Be open and honest about your feelings. I'm not sure why, but it seems to get harder for some couples to share their feelings with each other - the longer they are together. You would think it would get easier, but not so. The fact is that in order for a relationship to work, there must be open communication about everything, not just about who is going to pick up Suzie from the counsellor's office, and who should follow up on the child's safety plan. When you're talking about the things that matter, it is imperative that you share how you feel, and what you want.

If you don't say these things, your partner will not be able to read your mind no matter how long you've been together. You need to take responsibility for your wants, needs, thoughts, opinions, and feelings - and share them with your partner. S/he needs to do the same. Remove all doubt, and just say it like it is. Remember to OWN your feelings. Don't lay blame (see previous item) and say, "You make me..." - just say, "I feel... I need... I want... I think..." This is called "*sharing*", and if you remember - you used to do this all the time when you were dating. This is why you felt so connected, and why you decided to go ahead and make it official. Now that you are together in a "committed" relationship - you can't toss those communication tools out the window. You need them more than ever.

You'll notice that one word keeps recurring in this section: the word BEFORE. Ensuring that your partnership stays anger-proof is all about being proactive. If you anticipate what challenges could throw a monkey wrench into your relationship, and attack it head on before it creeps up on you, you have a much better chance of preserving your partnership. Openness, honesty, vulnerability, and humility are all keys to making a love relationship work. Most relationships fail due to lack of communication - so get those lines open, and keep them open. Stuffing your anger inside will only cause you to become sick, bitter, and lonely in your relationship. Truth is: the love you think you have lost is in your house, probably stuffed under a sofa cushion, or tucked away in a box of love letters in the basement. It is there - and has been all along. By opening up your communication, and planning to play together, you can get it back before it's too late.

12

The Cost of Playing Games

Bullying is not a playground activity that can be dismissed as a normal feature of childhood. The stakes are too high, with grave emotional and physical consequences. Individuals who are bullied are not only deprived of nearly all the joy in living but also have a significantly elevated risk of suicide.

Sometimes the direct and indirect costs of providing appropriate treatment for a bullied child may be prohibitive for a family with limited finances. Additional financial burdens such as taking time off work, or providing transportation to and from treatment can be extremely taxing to the point that some families opt out of treatment.

> **Laurie:** The human cost to the victims and their families is so vast as to be immeasurable in terms of dollars and cents. In our case, the combined monetary cost to the education and health care system, and our family has easily exceeded $75,000.00.

Our Case: The Cost of Bullying

Direct Medical Interventions/ Treatment	Frequency of Visits	Expense
Emergency Room	Approximately 10 visits@ $260	$2600
One week stay in hospital (private room)	7 days@$2500	$17500
Ambulance - Police/fire/paramedic	2 rides @ $240 each Plus (2 police, 8 fire fighters, 2 EMS workers)	$480 + fire/police manpower costs
Family physician	Approximately 25 visits @ $32	$800
Psychologists	Private treatment 10 sessions @ $150	$1500
Family therapist	Private Counselling	$3000
Contact Niagara Services	For Intake and Referral 2 Intakes, questionnaires, and referrals, approximately $300 each	$600.00
Psychiatrist Assessment and Treatment	**Frequency/ Duration**	**Expense**
Assessments	Psychiatrist Private assessment	$2000 $2000

School Services		Expense
Social worker – Grade 8	10 meetings along with transportation @ $28/hr	$280
Social skills class – Grade 8	In-class workshops – after bullying	Est. $200
Home school - 1 semester, Grade 9	6 months @ $84/hour/week	Est. $2016
Home school -1 semester, Grade 12	6 months @ $84/hour/week	Est. $2016
Youth worker high school	Numerous Meetings!	Est. $2000
Drugs and Alternative Healing		**Expense**
Allergy specialists, Niagara & Hamilton	6 visits @ $105	$630
Arthritis specialist	2 visits @ $105	$210
Neurology	2 visits @ $105	$210
Specialist visits to McMaster	7 visits @ $260	$1820 (Does not include specialist fees)
Lab tests – MRI/CAT	MRI $641 CAT $650	$1291
Parental Lost Wages	6 months (Sick leave, time off without pay)	Personal
*Total Direct and Indirect Costs:		**$77, 243**

*Please note: These are estimated costs. Since OHIP covers many of the expenses in its universal package, the non-insured resident rates were used in some cases.

Many of these expenses could have been saved, and the complications noted could have been avoided had the bullying been addressed in its early stages. But what is the cost to the family whose child never emerges from the crisis?

There is no doubt in my mind that schools must encourage and train those working with kids to handle relational problems in a positive manner. Handling bullying or other undesirable behaviours negatively can escalate bullying, causing it to go underground or to deteriorate relationships even further. Teachers or principals who yell at the bullies in front of others do not prevent or help the situation. They perpetuate more bullying through their own inappropriate attempt to deal with it.

Families cannot and should not be expected to solve this social and relational challenge on their own. Families, educators, health professionals and community partners need to work hard, together, in order to ensure that no child of tomorrow has to endure the same experience as those who are bullied today.

13

Coaches' Comments

As mentioned in the previous chapter, there are a myriad of resources and services in your community that are available to assist with supporting bullied children. This book would not be complete if it did not share some examples of such resources with you. This chapter is comprised of valuable information provided by dedicated professionals who care about the bullying issue and have unique perspectives on how to handle it. First, we will hear from Bonnie Prentice of TALK (Teams of Adults Listening to Kids), followed by Way2Click with tips on responding to cyber bullying. Lastly, the John Howard Society of Niagara offers information about school mediation programs between bullies and their victims.

TALK (Teams of Adults Listening to Kids)

Contributed by Bonnie Prentice

TALK, a regional project addressing the issue of youth victimization, is a partnership including the Niagara Regional Police Service, Niagara Catholic District School Board, Ecole secondaire Jean Vanier, District School Board of Niagara, Niagara Child and Youth Services, FORT, Rainbow Youth Niagara, RAFT, Ecole secondaire Confederation, Niagara Region Public Health and YLC Cura Niagara as consulting partners.

Since 2004, TALK has endeavoured to support school and community efforts to reduce/eliminate bullying, harassment, dating violence, racism, homophobia, and transphobia; to provide information and resources related to youth victimization and to impress upon educators and professionals working with children and youth that bullying and youth victimization have lifelong consequences for both victims and perpetrators; and, furthermore, the inclusion of youth engagement and school/community-wide responses as essential in changing the culture of youth victimization.

Observations from the work of TALK:

- The size of the student population, location of the school, and socio-economic status of the youth are not relevant to the degree of safety experienced by students.

- Anyone can be targeted and become a victim of bullying.

- Students identified the need for activities designed to help the student body to bond and reduce cliques; such activities are essential for reducing youth victimization.

- Students identified cyber bullying and the spreading of rumours as the most severe problem, and indicated that there should be more education to help young people understand the seriousness of this issue.

- Victimization can take many forms, but homophobic bullying is the constant, and is usually included in bullying of any kind. It is also often ignored by teachers.

- Students attending schools with a student-led, staff supported Safe School Committee, Anti-bullying Group, Diversity Group, and/or Gay-

Straight Alliance expressed the highest feelings of safety and felt most positive about their teachers and administrators.

- Educators and other professionals working with youth need training in order to respond effectively to serious incidents of bullying.

- "One-off" school assemblies about bullying have no lasting effect, unless they are followed up on in the classroom throughout the entire year.

- Students report that adult silence = endorsement of the behaviour. Thus, an adult's reaction does not have to be big; there just has to be one.

- Schools should set up their Safe School club just like any other regular expected club (student council, drama club, choir, band, etc.) – they should meet regularly, have a clear agenda, take yearbook pictures, and be featured with all the other clubs/groups in the school.

- Safe space messages should be everywhere – from curriculum to change rooms, to busses and hallways. All the staffs need to be on board. Expectations about bullying need to be the same as any other expectation about curriculum completion or school conduct.

- Parents must be included in any anti-victimization efforts related to children and youth.

TALK has been funded by the Ministry of the Attorney General and is currently funded by the Ontario Trillium Foundation. The views and opinions expressed in this publication do not necessarily reflect those of the Government of Ontario.

Tips from Way2Click: How to Respond to Cyber bullying

Your first tactic should be to use your head. Cyber bullying is a lot easier to prevent than it is to fix. If it is too late for that, it might be easiest to just delete your current email accounts, cell phone/pager accounts, and set up new ones.

Never give out or share your personal information. That includes your name, the names of friends or family, your address, phone number, and school name. Personal information also includes pictures of yourself and/or your email address. Never share your passwords!

Be polite to others online just as you would offline. If someone treats you rudely, don't respond. Online bullies are just like offline ones – they WANT you to answer. Don't give them the satisfaction.

Never send a message to others when you are angry. Wait until you have had time to calm down and think. Once you have sent a message, it is nearly impossible to undo whatever damage your message causes.

Never open a message from someone you do not know.

Turn off, disconnect, and unplug. Give yourself a break. You do not have to be available 24/7.

Don't reply to messages from cyber bullies, even though you may really want to. Cyber bullies want to know that they are messing with your mind.

Most importantly, do not erase or delete messages sent to you from cyber bullies. You don't have to read them, but it is advisable that you keep them, along with the date stamp, and where they were sent from. It can take a lot of time and effort to get Internet service providers (ISPs) and mobile telecommunications service providers to respond and deal with your complaints about being cyber bullied. Nevertheless, the police, your ISP, and/or your telephone company can use this information to help you bring the cyber bullies to justice.

This information was provided courtesy of www.way2click.com and www.b-free.ca. They can be reached in the Niagara Region at 905-714-9815, and in the Greater Toronto Area, 416-619-7941.

John Howard Society of Niagara
Project Rewind: School Based Prevention

Repairing the harm
"Focus is on the actions, rather than the actors"

Project REWIND at the John Howard Society of Niagara is a school based prevention program funded by the Ministry of Child and Youth Services. The program focuses on Restoring Events with Integrity, Negotiation and Dignity. Project REWIND works in partnership with Niagara schools both elementary and secondary in different school boards across the Niagara Region, as well as Contact Niagara and the Niagara Regional Police Service. Project REWIND is responding proactively to harming behaviour by mediating restorative conferences.

Project REWIND began in the Niagara Region in May of 2007. This program is based on a restorative justice program developed in 1970 in New Zealand to begin victim/offender reconciliation. Restorative approaches to crime have been used in many countries dating back thousands of years. With the change from the Young Offenders Act to the Youth Criminal Justice Act communities have begun to use different approaches to responding to youth offences. A restorative approach focuses on the affects crime has on people, relationships and the community.

Project REWIND mediators use a scripted tool to run restorative conferences, encourage the development of an agreement and follow up. This conference provides an opportunity for all individuals affected by an incident to be heard, be a part of behaviour change, healing, reparation and rebuilding of relationships and community. Since May of 2007, more than 300 restorative conferences have been run by Project REWIND Mediators. Restorative conferences are run in response to issues such as:

- Bullying (physical, emotional, mental, cyber)
- Racial and cultural confrontation
- Relationship difficulties/harassment
- Minor assaults and fighting
- Stealing
- Vandalism
- Truancy

What are the Goals of Mediation?

The Mediation Conference only focuses on one specific incident of harming behaviour. It does not seek to fix blame, or determine who is "good" or "bad", but affirms the integrity and respect of all the participants. Its goals include:

✓ A safe opportunity to express genuine feelings, concerns, hurts and apologies.

• • •

- ✓ Those harmed have an opportunity to be heard.
- ✓ Those harmed and those responsible for the harm are involved in determining what can repair and prevent further harm.
- ✓ Those responsible for the harm are encouraged to think through their actions.
- ✓ To increase awareness and understanding of the full impact of the harming behaviour.
- ✓ To enhance the dignity and respect of all participants.
- ✓ To empower everyone involved with the opportunity to play a significant role in 'healing the harm'.
- ✓ To develop an "Agreement" to which all participants can sign and commit.
- ✓ To affirm a strong sense of safety and care to the school community.
- ✓ To provide a powerful learning experience.
- ✓ To support "positive closure".

Who is involved?

It is important to note that the Mediation Conference is strictly voluntary and no one is pressured to participate.

The participants include:

- ✓ The person or persons harmed.
- ✓ The person or persons who are responsible for the harm and who willingly acknowledge responsibility for the incident.
- ✓ Other persons who have been impacted by the harming in some way and are willing to support the procedure.

Referral Process

The referrals come into the program through a variety of sources. The school referrals come from designated individuals within each school. Some of these individuals may include, but are not limited to: Principals, Vice Principals, Student Success Teachers, Guidance Counsellors as well as Teachers.

In some cases there have also been self referrals from the actual students themselves. In a self referral situation, the Program Coordinator of Project REWIND would discuss the referral with the designate at the school to inquire if they feel the student should participate in the program.

Project REWIND also receives referrals from Contact Niagara based on Extrajudicial Measures. Extrajudicial measures are ways that young people can be diverted or kept out of the youth criminal justice system. If the police decide to use one of these measures, they will not lay a charge against you and you will not have to go to court. Some extrajudicial measures allow you and people who have been affected by your actions to participate in the decision-making.

Extrajudicial measures are used when an adolescent commits an offence for the first time and the offence is non-violent. Youth who have been involved in an extra judicial measure in the past and have been successful may also be offered the opportunity to participate, as long as they are adequate to hold the adolescent accountable for his behaviour. These referrals are first provided by the Niagara Regional Police who then in turn send the file to the Youth Justice Coordinator to approve. After the file is approved it then is sent on to Contact Niagara who completes an intake with the youth and their family and then sends it to Project REWIND.

When a referral is received either by a school or Contact Niagara a meeting is set up with the referral source to receive more information on the situation.

• • •

During this meeting all parties identify their role in the situation. Information is gathered on the occurrence as well as the events leading up to it. This part of the process is imperative since it provides the facilitator with the instruction on how to move forward with the mediation.

The next step would be to complete a pre-conference interview with all youth involved in the situation. The Offender or Harmer is always interviewed first. The reason behind this is to ensure that they have accepted responsibility for their actions and not to re-victimize the victim. If at any point, during this meeting the individual does not accept responsibility the mediation or conference will not take place and the referral source will be informed. It is important to note that the process is strictly voluntary for all parties involved. If an individual does not want to participate, for any reason they do not have to.

In some cases if the process does not move forward the school, police or Contact Niagara may opt to use further disciplinary action. The individuals, depending on their roles are asked specific questions pertaining to the occurrence. At the completion of all of the pre-conference meetings all of the individuals involved are brought together to complete the conference process. It should be noted that the questions asked during the pre-conference interviews are asked again in the conference. The reason behind this is that the pre-conference interviews are a time for information gathering whereas during the actual conference the answers are given in order for the other side to learn how the behaviour has affected the other person or persons. At the completion of the conference, an agreement form is drawn up and signed by all participants. What is put on the agreement is entirely up to the participants of the conference. The only stipulation is that everyone must agree to the terms. A copy is provided to all parties involved as well as the referral source. The Program Coordinator or facilitator follows up on the conference 2 weeks later to ensure that the agreement is being followed.

Feedback from previous participants

"This was an awesome way of dealing with the situation" ~*Parent of victim*

"Excellent process – very helpful"
~*Parent of offender*

"I feel the situation was fixed and I am happy with the result"
~*Victim*

For more information

Project REWIND is in many elementary and secondary schools across the Niagara Region; however, it is not available in all schools. If your school is not currently using the process and as a staff member or parent, you would like more information on the program, the Program Coordinator will be more than happy to provide more information both verbally and in a hard copy form.

For further information about Project Rewind, please contact,
John Howard Society of Niagara
210 King Street
St. Catharines, ON
Phone (905) 682-2657 ext 258
Fax (905) 984-6918

14

Injuries and Trauma Recovery: Messages from the Field

Amanda could not have made the strides in recovery that she did without the help and committed support of a team of caring professionals. One such individual is Erinne Andrews, Amanda's Art Therapist. In the pages that follow, Erinne shares her unique perspective of Amanda's journey. Erinne's commentary is followed by our final thoughts as well as a last word from Amanda.

Amanda was fourteen when she was referred to a children's mental health clinic to address her experiences with bullying at school. At the time of referral, Amanda had already seen several other professionals to address these experiences but was still struggling with anxiety, depression and attending school. Although Amanda was able to continue with after school activities, she was unable to get to school, suffering with headaches, migraines, inability to get to sleep at night and subsequent difficulty getting up in the morning. These contradictions in functioning were confusing and frustrating for Amanda as well as her parents. Arguments and conflict increased at home and her relationship with her parents at home was strained.

Both Amanda and her parents appeared to be at a loss for what to do next.

It appeared previous treatment focused on decreasing anxiety, depression and increasing school attendance through the use of cognitive behavioural strategies (CBT) without assessing the possibility that anxiety, depression, school attendance problems may have been signs and symptoms that Amanda's experiences with her bullies had produced trauma. According to Steele (1999) 'the longer a trauma victim goes without trauma-specific help the more chronic and severe the reactions can become." Without assessing and providing treatment for trauma, Amanda's overall psycho-social-emotional well being was at risk as trauma signs and symptoms worsened and family functioning was deteriorating. A shift in treatment focus would include psycho-education regarding bullying as a trauma experience, individual trauma work, and informing Amanda and her parents about trauma.

Bullying is commonly written off as a 'soft form of abuse' as many of us has experienced cruelty at school and lived to 'tell the tale' (Anthes, 2010). However, if abuse causes physical, psychological and emotional harm (as is caused by bullying), then one would conclude that bullying is abuse and abuse is traumatic. At the core of trauma is terror, an overwhelming sense of powerlessness and fear for one's own safety (Steele, 1999). Amanda was terrified to go to school; the fear of the occurrence of verbal and physical assaults was constant, and she felt powerless to change what was happening at school. Not only was her own personal safety compromised, her safe place of school, her social community, her place to belong, to learn and excel, and to make friends became a place of terror. Friendships that were once rich with safety, comfort, laughter, and fun became the source of her terror. Amanda found herself in a paradox, understanding that she 'had to' attend school and knowing that she couldn't. Attachment researchers, Mary Main and Erik Hesse have observed similar reactions in children whose pattern of attachment are insecure and disorganized (as cited in Siegel and Hartzell, 2004). They refer to this as "'fright without solution', an unsolvable dilemma for a child who can find no way to make sense of a situation or develop an organized adaptation" (p. 106). Her 'unsolvable dilemma' was wrapped with sadness, grief and loss of her sense of belonging, identity and relationships.

Trauma is also defined by Alvarado (2008) as any stressful experience that is overwhelming, fearful, and not within our control (p 15). To be bullied is stressful, it is fear producing, and it is not within our control. Trauma interrupts the development of the regulation system leaving us dysregulated (p.37). Alvarado elaborates on dysregulation:

> Dysregulation in the brain looks like: confused and distorted thinking, poor reasoning skills, diminished cognitive capacity, and limited ability for abstract thought or at times concrete thought.

> Dysregulation in the body looks like: defensive posture, poor eye contact, poor motor regulation, hyper active/aroused behaviours, appetite and sleep disturbances, inappropriate sexual behaviour, tension, altered blood pressure-heart rate-body temperature, physical aches and pains.

> Dysregulation in the mind/ soul looks like: poor social skills, emotional reactivity, lack of self esteem, lack of intimacy, lack of attachment and

connection to others, loneliness, isolation etc. (p. 32)

Amanda was unable to regulate, she was in a chronic state of fear and hypoarousal, and she was unable to function under the threat of going to school. An excerpt from Amanda's journal reads:

Dear Journal...
I'd rather die than go to school...
I'm going to throw up, I'm going to cry, and I'm going to get a migraine. No one understands what it feels like... I hate my mom and I hate my teachers don't they get that this is unbearable for me? Don't they get that going to school is the worst thing in the world? I never ever want to step foot in that building again... dragging me out of bed isn't helping anyone its only making me hate you more. Every time I go to school another piece of myself is ripped away, I'm not allowed to be me. I used to be happy, fun, and smart. Now I am an outcast, I am not liked, I am a

loser, I am ugly, and I am stupid. I'll never have friends again what is the point in continuing on?

It was also clear that Amanda had experienced prolonged exposure to traumatic and stressful events. Trauma has also been included in the DSM IV-TR, the Diagnostic and Statistical Manual of Mental Health Disorders, under the diagnosis of Post Traumatic Stress Disorder (PTSD). When trauma signs and symptoms persist for one month or more and interfere with daily function, a diagnosis of PTSD may be considered by a psychiatrist. The following are the criteria for PTSD:

A. The person has been exposed to a traumatic event in which both of the following were present:

- The person experienced, witnessed, or was confronted with an event or events that involved actual or threatened death or serious injury, or a threat to the physical integrity of self or others.

- The person's response involved intense fear, helplessness, or horror.

B. The traumatic event is persistently re-experienced in one (or more) of the following ways:

- recurrent and intrusive distressing recollections of the event, including images, thoughts, or perceptions;

- recurrent distressing dreams of the event;

- acting or feeling as if the traumatic event were recurring (includes a sense of reliving the experience, illusions, hallucinations, and dissociative flashback episodes, including those that occur on awakening or when intoxicated);

- intense psychological distress at exposure to internal or external cues that symbolize or resemble an aspect of the traumatic event;
- physiological reactivity on exposure to internal or external cues that symbolize or resemble an aspect of the traumatic event.

C. Persistent avoidance of stimuli associated with the trauma and numbing of general responsiveness (not present before the trauma), as indicated by three (or more) of the following:

- efforts to avoid thoughts, feelings, or conversations associated with the trauma;
- efforts to avoid activities, places, or people that arouse recollections of the trauma;
- inability to recall an important aspect of the trauma;
- markedly diminished interest or participation in significant activities;
- feeling of detachment or estrangement from others;
- restricted range of affect (e.g., unable to have loving feelings);
- sense of a foreshortened future (e.g., does not expect to have a career, marriage, children, or a normal life span).

D. Persistent symptoms of increased arousal (not present before the trauma), as indicated by two (or more) of the following:

- difficulty falling or staying asleep;
- irritability or outbursts of anger;
- difficulty concentrating;
- hyper vigilance;

- exaggerated startle response.

E. Duration of the disturbance (symptoms in Criteria B, C, and D) is more than 1 month.

F. The disturbance causes clinically significant distress or impairment in social, occupational, or other important areas of functioning.

'Trauma which occurs in the context of relationship can only be healed in the context of a relationship" (Alvarado, 2008, p.41). Healing is not a solitary journey. Everyone needs someone to bear witness to their experiences, to listen, and to care. Trauma recovery includes rebuilding trust, regaining confidence, returning to a sense of security, and reconnecting to love (Perry and Szalavitz, 2006).

What Can Help?

For Children and Adolescents:

1. To be trauma informed, to have their reactions normalized, validating their 'normal reactions' to an 'abnormal' and terrifying experience.

2. To engage in trauma informed therapeutic treatment with a well trained, skilled trauma expert. Treatment will focus on physical, psychological stabilization, re-establishing safety and security, emotional regulation strategies, reintegration of the effects of trauma experiences and reconstruction of self and relationships.

3. For parents/caregivers to be trauma informed, to be well regulated, loving, consistent and attuned, parenting from a trauma informed perspective. A trauma informed, well regulated parent will be able to remain attuned to their child's emotional state and respond vs. react. (Alvarado, 2008).

4. For parents/caregivers to be committed to family healing, not child healing. (Alvarado, 2008)

5. For parents/caregivers, professionals and educators to work together to re-establish school as a safe place, facilitate safe, caring and supportive peer relationships.

6. To have a rich, social community, in school and outside of school.

Perry and Szalavitz (2006) strongly believe that even with the best medications and therapy in the world, healing is impossible without lasting, caring connections.

For Parents and Caregivers:

1. Have a deep understanding of the impact of your own history, fear and stress (Alvarado, 2008). Seek out your own personal (couple) trauma informed therapy to maintain regulation and understanding. "You cannot do for others what you cannot do for yourself".

2. Become trauma informed. Develop a deep understanding of trauma and the effects of such on your child, self, your relationships, your marriage and your family.

3. Respond vs. React (Alvarado, 2008) Think carefully about how your responses may impact your child's emotions, or what consequences might be produced by your actions today. Seek to do what is in the best interests of your child and your family both for now, and down the road.

4. Recognize your child/teen's competency to direct his/her own treatment and self care. Remain attuned, loving, consistent, and caring. Recovery requires your child/teen to be in charge of key aspects of therapeutic intervention to regain a sense of control, safety and power that was taken away through their trauma experiences (Perry and Szalavitz, 2006).

5. Work together with the education system and other professionals, advocating for what is best for your child. You are the expert! Next to your own child/teen, you know them the best!

6. Parent together. Your child's healing and your healing is dependent on having healthy, strong and caring relationships.

7. Facilitate and support socially rich experiences and environments for your teen/child. When school is unsafe, when relationships at school have injured, your child/teen needs "anything that will increase the number and quality of their relationships".

"Because humans are inescapably social beings, the worst catastrophes that can befall us inevitably involve relational loss" (p. 231). Bullying behavior attacks what we do best: relationships. Bullying is not a rite of passage, just because as adults we have survived these experiences does not make it right that these experiences continue. We cannot accept it as a part of human nature or of 'kids being kids'. Healing requires patience, self recovery and relationship recovery. It is possible!

Dear Journal...
BULLIES, you can't make
me feel like you did in
grade 8. I am strong
now. Take all my friends
away I'm still
unbreakable... you can't
take away my pride, my
confidence. I am a good
person and I will be
successful because of it.
People don't make me
happy I make myself

happy. You have no
POWER over me. I have
my mom and dad and
grandma, those are the
people that matter and
they will love and
support me no matter
what. I can go to school
because you have no
right to take that away
from me. **Amanda.**

I offer my kind thanks to Amanda for having the courage to share. I am honored to have witnessed her journey. Erinne Andrews, B.A., A.T. Dipl., Art Therapist.

Julie: When Laurie and I started down this road, we both agreed that while writing the book was a good idea, it would not be enough. Out of our discussions and rough notes, we developed a school session that we have facilitated within elementary schools in the Niagara Region. We are always humbled and thankful when the children let us know that our presentation has affected them in some positive way. We are even more grateful when some participant in our session will step forward and say, "I am being bullied at school." Our response is always the same – we encourage and share some helpful tips with the child, notify the teacher immediately, and share some suggestions with the teacher, and then ask for some feedback as to the welfare of the child later on.

I believe that the most powerful aspect of our presentation is the point at which we share with the children the importance of making choices for themselves as opposed to just going along with the crowd. We then read this beautiful message that Amanda wrote to students anywhere and everywhere, who have come in contact with bullying. It is a message of hope, recovery, strength, and resilience; one that truly resonates with the hearts and minds of those who listen.

You Have a Choice

Dear Friend,

I was bullied when I was in grade 8. It hurt me very badly. I am now in University and I have friends. I didn't think that would happen when I was your age. My mom and dad told me it would and it did.

I have a message for all of you today. You're going to hear me use the word, "choice" because every action each one of you takes is a choice.

First off if you're a **bully,** my message to you is you are NOT worth anything more than anyone else and no one is worth MORE than you. Don't try to make yourself feel better by making someone else feel bad. We can choose to use our power for something positive. Make change; help make this world a great place. You have a chance to help your neighbour feel good or put them down;

my question to you is, what do you choose?

To the **bystander**: you have the biggest opportunity to become a leader. If we choose to sit and watch when we know that bullying is happening, the hurt we cause is just as bad as the hurt the bully causes. When you see someone being mean to someone else and you know deep in your heart that it's wrong, listen to that little voice inside. Don't go along with the rest of the crowd; it is not cool to be mean. It's cooler to be a friend to someone who needs a friend.

To the person who has been or is being **bullied**: IT IS NOT YOUR FAULT. You choose to become strong. You choose the messages you tell yourself. You choose to say, "I am a good person and I do not deserve this". You choose to do something positive rather than continue to let yourself hurt. Don't let anyone tell you you're not worth it. Because everyone is so worth it.

Moms and Dads: we all try to do the best we can. During the time it will take to end bullying, you will come into contact with and spend time trying to work with many different types of people. It is helpful to remember that at some time or another, we all make mistakes, and we often don't know *what to do. Some of the frustrations or setbacks won't amount to much if, at the end of your involvement in the bullying situation, you know that your child is safe.*

Laurie: Sometime after we had come out the other side of bullying, and Amanda was well into her recovery, she sent me the following poem in an Email message. You cannot imagine how it felt, after years of struggling, worrying, crying, and fearing for my daughter, to receive this ray of hope and sunshine beaming from the heart of my daughter. Bullies think that they can strip you of everything that you are, and turn you into something that exists only for their pleasure. I believe it was Eleanor Roosevelt who said, "No one can make you feel small without your permission." Now we know this to be true – no one can steal your dignity, your self-respect, or your hope for the future without your permission. I am so proud of Amanda for taking back her life and for refusing to give the bullies permission to harm her anymore. May her words lighten your load and give you hope as they did for me.

• • •

Mom,
I don't know this person, this old/ new
stranger.
This person who was once low, once sad,
once gone astray.
Who were you? Who am I?
I am learning.
I am happy. Happier than EVER.
I am someone's friend,
I am someone's girlfriend,
Most of all people like me, people besides
you and dad.
Mom, I'm going to school, I never miss a
day!
But besides that, I LOVE going to school.
(never ever thought I'd ever say that ha
ha!)
I could cry I'm so happy...
I'm really going to be ok.
I'm really going to make something of my
life.
I can allow myself to let you be proud of
me, because for once I'M PROUD OF MYSELF.
I've never felt more confident.
I've never been surer that who I am
becoming is good.
I've never felt more successful.
I never thought this day was going to
come; it was so hard to believe in...
I had some faith, and I had some help...
And here I am, a brand new girl. I'm
beginning to actually like ME.

• • •

Thanks for helping me get here!
I love you.

Appendix A: Planning Tools and Checklists

School Checklist

This checklist might aid you in making an assessment of how your school is responding to the issue of bullying.

Our school Has:	Inadequate	Adequate	Outstanding
1. Acquired useful resources for educating the school community about bullying			
2. Taken steps to gather facts about bullying at your school			
3. Developed school policy by involving staff, students and parents			
4. Produced an anti-bullying or safe school policy			
5. Ensured that staff have discussed bullying with students			

Our school Has:	Inadequate	Adequate	Outstanding
6. Ensured that victimized students have been supported			
7. Ensured that incidents of bullying have been handled and positively resolved			
8. Recognized students who have helped resolve bullying issues			
10. Held meetings with parents on issues of bullying			
11. Make plans to review the bullying prevention work			
12. A set response time (e.g. 8 hours) for reporting of bullying incidents that is adhered to			

Our school Has:	Inadequate	Adequate	Outstanding
13. Regular opportunities to brainstorm and collect ideas at staff meetings			
14. Walk-abouts throughout the school and playground at various times during the school day and year			
15. Surveys and questions distributed to teachers, staff, students and parents. Action plans to address results			

Our school Has:	Inadequate	Adequate	Outstanding
16. Researched all resources available in community (e.g. school mediation programs, children's mental health services, police liaisons and supports, etc.), and accessed those that are appropriate.			
17. Ensured that teacher interventions have been supported by principal and school administration			

Bullying Occurrences in Less-Structured School Areas and Suggested Intervention Strategies

School Area	Suggested Intervention Strategies
Playground	• Increase supervision • Encourage co-operative games • Create out-of-bounds areas for places where visibility is difficult • Have extra playground monitors that have been trained on Bill 158, the signs of bullying, how to respond if you witness bullying, or are approached by a bullied child. These staff members should also be aware of school policies and procedures for dealing with bullying.
Lunchroom	• Increase supervision • Provide seating plans • Develop a consistent set of rules/expectations • Have student and parents sign a lunchroom contract

School Area	Suggested Intervention Strategies
Washroom	• Use a monitor • Restrict the number of students from classroom at one time • Develop a sign-out process with a record of time and who has left the classroom
School Bus	• Enforce rules for bus behaviour • Create a seating plan and readjust it as needed • Develop a monitor/buddy system
Internet/Telephone	• Enforce rules on school computers (sites/Email) • Implement no cell rule for school • Increase teacher supervision/monitoring of computer time
Hallway Interaction	• Increase supervision • Stagger passing times between classes

Peace Keeping Agreement

A peace keeping agreement may be a useful tool for teachers or parents to use with children who bully. This agreement is not intended for use between bullies and their victims. Children who bully are more likely to respond positively to a "contract" between themselves and individuals whom they perceive to be in a higher position of power or authority than themselves. Therefore, it is unlikely that children who bully would respect an agreement between themselves and persons whom they perceive to have less power. Here is an example of a Peace Keeping Agreement that you may incorporate into your bullying prevention strategies.

Peace Keeping Agreement

Date: _____

Peacekeepers
Name: _____
Name: _____

Challenge: _____
_____

Solution: _____
_____

Benefit: _____
_____

Signed: _____ Date: _____
Witnessed: _____ Date: _____

Example of How to Complete Your Peace Keeping Agreement:

You may want to begin a short discussion with the child/young person about what is happening and why s/he is choosing to bully another child. Remember that some bullies lack empathy, so a lengthy discussion about how the other child feels may not likely yield positive results. Focus your attention on how bullying is affecting the bully in negative ways (e.g. feel guilty, don't have a lot of friends, suspensions or other consequences at school, disciplinary action at home). If the bully has not received many negative consequences for his/her behaviour, discuss the potential outcomes if bullying continues (e.g. arrests, expulsion from school, loss of status or power in the school environment, repercussions at home, and future ability to obtain employment because of criminal record, etc.). Explore the positive outcomes of treating the target(s) of bullying with respect – or just leaving them alone.

Invite the child to participate in a contract with you. Show the child the contract and explain that this contract will be enforceable for a limited time (say, 15 days). Work with the child to summarize what the presenting challenge is.

E.g. Challenge: "I pick on Jimmy by teasing him, punching him, and getting my friends to ignore him at break times. I get in trouble for this and have been suspended two times this year."

Then discuss possible solutions for the challenge.

E.g. Solution: "When I see Jimmy, I will decide that picking on him is not worth getting in more trouble. I will go somewhere else on the school grounds to play with my friends. When I feel like teasing Jimmy, I will

• • •

remember that if I don't have something nice to say, I should say nothing."

Finally, work with the child to make a list of the benefits of adhering to the contract.

E.g. Benefits: "By resisting the urge to bug Jimmy I will not get in trouble as much at school. People will like me more because I will not be seen as a mean person."

Of course, be sure to make the wording age-appropriate! Have the student sign the document, and you witness it as the adult. Be sure to check in with the child who bullies regularly to see how s/he is doing with adhering to the contract. When the contract expires, write up a new one. Continue to do so until the child has demonstrated the ability to self-regulate bullying behaviours.

Appendix B: Resources

Supports for Your Child and Your Family

School
Contact your local school as well as the school board in your area. They may offer many excellent programs that you may be unaware of. Talk to other teachers, parents, and stay in contact with your school parent council.

Your local Church or Place of Worship
Many places of worship will offer counselling, small group support, pastoral care, and/or specialized workshops.

Hospital Programs
Each hospital will have its own unique services, which may include children's mental health services. There may be a rich variety of hidden programs under this umbrella. We found a children's clinic with a specialized school program helping high school students to receive their education while getting specialized counselling. The hospital also offered a social skills program for elementary students. A six-week workshop for children who had been bullied and their parents was piloted and offered periodically. Many of the programs in your local hospital may be delivered based on need, the availability of community partnerships, and innovative initiatives by the hospital staff.

Crisis Care at your local hospital
A friendly understanding professional can help you and your child when a severe emotional emergency occurs. Some have phone-in services and others will provide in-person services. If you are concerned about suicide contact these services immediately or call 911.

Outreach Programs through Local Police
Contact the police and ask for information on services pertaining to youth and/or bullying. If you don't succeed the first time, try again. Often organizations like police departments can be so large, communication to the community about their specialized programming may be missed.

Employee Assistance
The counselling services provided through your employee assistance or benefits program may be a valuable resource, and may help with offsetting some of the out-of-pocket expenses associated with caring for your child and your family.

Local Distress Centres or Crisis Lines
Your community may have a crisis center or distress line that has supports available by telephone 24/7. Your child might also take advantage of Kids Help Phone or local phone-in services provided by children's mental health agencies.

Print Resources
In addition, there are a number of books you may find it worthwhile to read:

- *The Bully, the Bullied, and the Bystander* by Barbara Coloroso, published in 2003 by Collins Canada
- *Girl Wars: 12 Strategies That Will End Female Bullying* by Cheryl Dellasega, Ph.D. and

• • •

Charisse Nixon Ph.D. , published in 2003 by
Fireside
- *Mean Girls Gone: A Spiritual Guide to Getting
  Rid of Mean* by Hayley DiMarco published in
  2004 by Revell
- *Bully Proofing Your School: A Comprehensive
  Approach for Elementary Schools* by Garritty,
  Porter, Sager & Short-Camilli, published in
  2000 by Sopris West
- *Bullying at School: What we Know and What
  We Can Do* published in 1993 by Dan Olweus
- *The Wounded Spirit* by Frank Peretti, published
  in 2001
- *Stop the Bullying: A Handbook for Schools* by
  Ken Rigby, published in 2003 by Acer Press
- *New Perspectives on Bullying* published in
  2002 by Ken Rigby, published in 2002 by
  Jessica Kingley Publishers
- *Odd Girl Out: The Hidden Culture of
  Aggression in Girls* by Rachel Simons,
  published in 2011 by Mariner Books
- *Bullying in the Schools and What to Do About
  It* published in 2004 by Ken Rigby
- *Stick a Geranium in Your Hat and Be Happy,*
  by Barbara Johnson, published in 2004 by
  Barbara Johnson
- *In Pursuit of Peace: 21 Ways to Conquer
  Anxiety, Fear, and Discontentment,* by Joyce
  Meyer, published in 2004 by Warner Faith

Internet Resources

There are many incredible sites that provide resources, information and support which can help you and your child at any point of your journey. We have listed a few for your consideration:

PREVNet
www.prevnet.ca
Debra Pepler is a Distinguished Research Professor of Psychology at York University (Toronto, Canada) and a Senior Associate Scientist at the Hospital for Sick Children. With Dr. Wendy Craig, she currently co-leads PREVNet (Promoting Relationships and Eliminating Violence Network; www.prevnet.ca). She is a world-respected authority on bullying research and provides advice on safe schools and contributes to advisory committees related to parenting, antisocial behaviour, and school violence. The PrevNet site contains many resources for parents, teachers, principals, children, youth, recreation leaders, bus drivers etc.

Way2Click
www.way2click.com
Way2click is an Internet Safety & Support Solutions providing Internet safety options for home and school use.

Distress Centres of Ontario
www.dcontario.org
Provides a 24-hour crisis line in communities across the province of Ontario

Centre for Suicide Prevention
www.suicideinfo.ca
The Centre for Suicide Prevention (CSP) is a not for profit education centre affiliated with Canadian Mental Health Association (CMHA). CSP offers training (community workshops and online courses) and has the

largest English language library dedicated to the collection and dissemination of suicide prevention, intervention and post-vention resources.

Pathstone Mental Health
www.pathstonementalhealth.ca
Niagara Regions Children's Mental Health services (each community has their own children's mental health services that will deal with bullying and the traumatic affects)

Canadian Mental Health Association
www.cmha.ca
Promotes mental health of all and supports the resilience and recovery of people experiencing mental illness.

CAMH – Centre for Addictions and Mental Health
www.camh.net
Provides articles and current research on bullying

211
www.211canada.ca
211 is an easy to remember telephone number that connects people to a full range of non-emergency social, health and government services in their community. Twenty-four hours a day, seven days a week, trained counsellors answer 211 calls, assess the needs of each caller and link them to the best available information and services.

Canadian Safe School Network (CSSN)
www.canadiansafeschools.com
The Canadian Safe School Network (CSSN) is a national, charitable organization dedicated to reducing youth violence and making our schools and communities safer.

Kids Help Phone
www.kidshelpphone.ca
Kids Help Phone maintains a website called "Let's Talk About Bullying." It also contains a page for grown-ups with links to resources about bullying.

Ontario Ministry of Education Policies - Safe Schools
www.edu.gov.on.ca/eng/teachers/safeschools.html
The Ministry of Education has a Safe Schools Strategy that allows our children to learn in a safe and secure environment.

Canadian Parents Magazine Online
www.canadianparents.com
Blogging, expert advice about a variety of issues facing parents

Canadian Best Practices Portal
http://cbpp-pcpe.phac-aspc.gc.ca/topic/br-rlac/6/page/1
This site has 50+ evidence based programs for various aspects of violence prevention.

Social Skills Programming

Olweus (Ol-Vay-Us) Bullying Prevention Program – www.olweus.org
The *Olweus Bullying Prevention Program* is a whole-school program aimed at preventing or reducing bullying throughout a school setting. The *Olweus Bullying Prevention Program* is designed to improve peer relations and make schools safer, more positive places for students to learn and develop. Goals of the program include: reducing existing bullying problems among students, preventing new bullying problems, and achieving better peer relations at school.

Hazelden Publishing
www.hazelden.org
Hazelden is the leading publisher of evidence-based programs and curricula for students in kindergarten through high school. Visit their online bookstore to peruse their education and prevention resources, including social skills and bullying prevention programs.

Co-operative Learning

Cooperative learning is an instructional strategy that simultaneously addresses academic and social skill learning by students. It is a well-researched instructional strategy and has been reported to be highly successful in the classroom.

Kennesaw State University
http://edtech.kennesaw.edu/intech/cooperativelearnin g.htm
This site provides an overview of what cooperative learning is, how it works, and the situations in which it can help. Various cooperative learning exercises are

provided, and these can easily be implemented in a classroom setting.

Saskatoon Public School Online Learning Centre
http://olc.spsd.sk.ca/DE/PD/instr/strats/coop/
This site is full of rich resources to help teachers set up cooperative learning strategies and systems in their classrooms. The online learning centre is open to students, teachers, parents, and employees of Saskatoon Public Schools as well as to the virtual public.

ProTeacher Directory
http://www.proteacher.com/020014.shtml
The ProTeacher Directory provides a catalogue of Internet resources related to cooperative learning.

Therapeutic Models:
A Summary

Solution Focused Brief Therapy (SFBT) (often referred to as simply 'solution focused therapy' or 'brief therapy') is a type of talking therapy that focuses on what clients want to achieve through therapy rather than on the problem(s) that made them seek help. One of the key components or tools of SFBT is the Miracle Question, which re-directs the client towards thinking about how the problem will look once it is solved, and helps the client to reach inward for the answers they need to create their desired outcomes. You can learn more about SFBT by visiting this website: **http://www.solutionfocused.net**

Cognitive-Behavioural Therapy: A culmination of strategies derived from Cognitive Therapy, Behaviour Therapy and Rational Emotive Therapy, CBT proves useful in challenging limiting beliefs and identifying empowering ones. In CBT, the objective is often to identify irrational or maladaptive thoughts, assumptions and beliefs that are related to debilitating negative emotions and identify what it is about them that may be dysfunctional or just not helpful. This is done in an effort to reject the distorted tendencies and replace them with more realistic and self-helping alternatives. You can learn more by visiting: **http://www.beckinstitute.org/what-is-cognitive-behavioral-therapy**

Reality Therapy: "Since unsatisfactory or non-existent connections with people we need are the source of almost all human problems, the goal of reality therapy is to help people reconnect" (William Glasser Institute). One of the greatest gifts of Reality Therapy is "self-evaluation". Through self-evaluation clients can uncover their limiting beliefs and begin to shape new, more empowering belief systems and new behaviours. They can also monitor their behaviours more closely and make more informed and conscious choices because they are more aware of the triggers for their anger as well as the outcomes they truly desire. In effect, self-evaluation enables the client to behave more pro-actively than reactively to situations as they arise. A wealth of information on Reality Therapy is available at: **http://www.wglasser.com**

Narrative Therapy: "Narrative therapy is a respectful and collaborative approach to counselling and community work. It focuses on the stories of people's lives and is based on the idea that problems are manufactured in social, cultural and political contexts. Each person produces the meaning of their life from the stories that are available in these contexts. A wider meaning of narrative therapy relates significantly to a relatively recent way of thinking about the nature of human life and knowledge which has come to be known as 'postmodernism' – which believes there is no one objective 'truth' and that there are many multiple possible interpretations of any event" (Narrative Therapy Centre of Toronto). You can learn more about Narrative Therapy by visiting: **www.narrativetherapycentre.com.**

Structural Family Therapy (SFT) is "similar to other types of therapies categorized under the psychological framework of family systems therapy. These types of therapies view the family unit as a system that lives and operates within larger systems, such as a culture, the community, and organizations. This system – ideally – grows and changes over time. But sometimes a family gets "stuck," often resulting from behavioural or mental health issues of one of its family members. Rather than focus on the individual's pathology, however, SFT considers problems in the family's structure - a dysfunction in the way the family interacts or operates. SFT does not maintain that the family's interactions, or "transactions" cause the pathology, but rather that the family's transactions support or encourage the symptoms" (All Psychology Careers). Learn more about SFT at **http://www.allpsychologycareers.com/topics/st ructural-family-therapy.html**

Art and Music Therapies: Art therapy is a tool that enables children, teens, and adults to express their feelings of stress, anxiety, grief, anger, etc., in a creative way. Art can help people to release their feelings in a way that is empowering and healing. Likewise, music therapy is a way for people to express their emotions either through the listening and interpretation of music, or through the expression of music through composition and experimentation. Therapeutic experiences may include singing, song writing, performing, or improvisation with one's voice or with instruments. It is not necessary for a participant to have any background or experience in music.

What is the difference between the following providers?

Psychiatrist
A psychiatrist is a medical doctor with a specialization in assessment and treatment of mental disorders as defined by the DSM IV-TR or the ICD-10 diagnostic systems. As a medical doctor, a psychiatrist is able to prescribe medications, and his/her services would be covered under a universal health care plan such as OHIP in Ontario. Some psychiatrists also provide talk therapy, but most focus primarily on assessment, diagnosis, and medical interventions (pharmaceutical treatment).

Psychologist/Psychological Associate
Psychologists typically have a Ph.D. in clinical psychology and are specialists in assessment and treatment of DSM IV-TR/ICD-10 disorders. Psychological Associates may have a Masters Degree or a Ph.D. in psychology and several hundred hours of supervised practice by a Psychologist. Psychologists and Psychological Associates provide talk therapy, but will differ in their approach depending on the theoretical model they prefer (e.g. CBT vs. SFT). Psychology is a regulated profession in most provinces and states.

Social Worker
Social work is a regulated profession in the province of Ontario and in many other provinces and states. Social workers may take on various roles, one of which may include counselling. Social workers may also assist with referral, helping with transitions and placement, and community access coordination.

You may also be referred to people who work as **counsellors** or **mental health workers** within organizations such as the CMHA or other community mental health services. They are able to provide valuable services in problem solving, planning, and coping with specific mental health issues.

About the Authors

Laurie Flasko, CSP

Laurie Flasko, CSP is a wife, daughter, sister, and friend but her most important accomplishment is mom to a beautiful successful young woman. She is also a professional speaker, coach and trainer with twenty years of experience in the fields of leadership, customer service, and teambuilding. Genuinely committed to the success of others, she inspires her audiences to reach for the extraordinary. Laurie is Certified Speaking Professional and a member of Canadian Speakers Association as well as the National Speakers Association.

www.laurieflasko.com

Julie A. Christiansen, M.A.

An internationally recognized speaker, and published author, Julie Christiansen brings close to 20 years experience in group and individual counselling. Branded as "Oprah for the Office" and "The Anger Lady" by her clients, she has been compared to the likes of Brian Tracy and Jack Canfield. She holds a B.A. in Psychology and a M.A. in Counselling Psychology, and teaches Psychology at George Brown College. Julie created the Anger Solutions™ Program, which is now in use in several cities across Canada and internationally. As an expert on anger and stress, Julie is a sought after guest expert for print, television, and radio media. Her passion lies in helping people to create *radical, positive, and lasting change* through her coaching, training, and corporate programs – all provided by her company, Leverage U. She is the author of six books including: *Anger Solutions, When the Last Straw Falls: 30 Ways to Keep Stress from Breaking Your Back,* and *Anger Solutions by the Book.*

www.juliechristiansen.com

www.angersolution.com

● ● ●
203

Credits and Thanks

We wish to express our thanks to the following individuals/organizations who contributed their knowledge and expertise to this work. We would also like to thank those Internet resources and authors who gave us permission to use their words:

1. Amanda Flasko

2. Barbara Eade, District School Board of Niagara

3. Barbara Coloroso

4. Bonnie Prentice, TALK Niagara

5. Dr. Debra Pepler

6. Dee Tyler, Executive Director, Distress Centre Niagara

7. Erinne Andrews, Art Therapist

8. Joan Hyatt, Jericho Counselling

9. John Howard Society of Niagara

10. Nadine Wallace, Niagara Regional Police Service

11. Way2Click.com

12. Zig Ziglar and Tom Ziglar

Endnotes

[i] CBC News. (2007). Quebec boy dies after schoolyard shoving match: Girl, 11, placed in care of child-protection services. *CBC News*, November 12, 2007. Retrieved from http://www.cbc.ca/canada/montreal/story//2007/11/12/qc-steeustachedeath1112.html

[ii] Valiante, G. (2009). Ontario teen convicted in rugby death. *National Post, May 28, 2009*. Retrieved from http://www.canada.com/news/teen+convicted+rugby+death/16392 46/story.html

[iii] Doucette, C. Bullies make girls' life a nightmare. *Toronto Sun.com*. May 6, 2010. Retrieved from http://www.torontosun.com/news/torontoandgta/2010/05/05/13839 771.html

[iv] Pepler, D., Craig, W. (2007). *Binoculars on bullying: A new solution to protect and connect children*. Voices for Children (www.voicesforchildren.ca), Feb. 2007. Used with permission.

[v] Pepler and Craig, 2007.

[vi] Birmaher, B., Boylan, K., & Romero, S. (2007). Psychopharmacologic treatment of pediatric major depressive disorder. *Psychopharmacology*, 191, 27-38.

[vii] Bowllan, N. M. (2011) Implementation and evaluation of a comprehensive, school-wide bullying prevention program in an urban/suburban middle school. Journal of School Health, 81(4), 167-173.

[viii] Birmaher, et al., 2007.

[ix] Bauman, S., Del Rio, A. (2006). Preservice Teachers' Responses to Bullying Scenarios: Comparing Physical, Verbal, and Relational Bullying. *Journal of Educational Psychology, 2006, Vol. 98, No. 1*, 219–23.

[x] Bauman and Del Rio, 2006.

[xi] Coloroso, B. (2008). *The bully, the bullied, and the bystander: From preschool to high school – how parents and teachers can help break the cycle*. New York: Harper Collins.

● ● ●

[xii] Harachi, Catalano, & Hawkins, 1999 as cited in Bauman and Del Rio, 2006.

[xiii] Bauman and Del Rio, 2006.

[xiv] Coloroso, B. (2008).

[xv] Hamarus, P., and Kaikkonen, P. (2008). School bullying as a creator of pupil peer pressure. *Educational research, Vol. 50:4.* Pp. 333-345.

[xvi] Craig, W., Peters, R.D., & Konarski, R. (1998). Bullying and victimization among Canadian school children (Catalogue no. W-98-28E). Ottawa: Human Resources Development Canada. Retrieved from http://publications.gc.ca/collections/collection_2008/hrsdc-rhdsc/MP32-28-98-28E.pdf

[xvii] Pepler, D., Craig, W. (2007).

[xviii] Full Esteem Ahead (n.d.). *Some reasons kids bully.* www.fullsteemahead.org. Retrieved from http://www.stopbullyingnow.com/Some reasons why kids bully.pdf

[xix] Bauman and Del Rio, 2006.

[xx] Bauman and Del Rio, 2006.

[xxi] Bauman and Del Rio, 2006.

[xxii] Jacobsen, K., Bauman, S. (2007). Bullying in Schools: School counsellors' responses to three types of bullying incidents. *Professional School Counseling, Vol. 11, Issue 1.*

[xxiii] Jacobsen and Bauman, 2007.

[xxiv] Birchmeier, Z., Flaspohler, P., Elfstrom, J., Vanderzee, K., Sink, H. (2009). Stand by me: The effects of peer and teacher support in mitigating the impact of bullying on quality of life. *Psychology in the Schools, Vol. 46, Issue 7:* 636-649.

[xxv] Canfield, J. (2005). *The Success Principles.* New York: Collins.

[xxvi] Peretti, F. (2000). *The Wounded Spirit.* USA: W Publishing Group.

[xxvii] Wood, Wood, Boyd, Wood, Desmarais, 2010.

[xxviii] Rivers, I., Noret, N. (2010). Participant roles in bullying

behaviour and their association with thoughts of ending one's life. *Crisis, Vol. 3, Issue 3:* 143-148.

[xxix] District School Board of Niagara. (2003). *Preventing Bullying in Our Schools.* District School Board of Niagara, Region 6.

[xxx] Pepler, D., Craig. W., 2007.

[xxxi] Dr. Dan Olweus is the founder and creator of the Olweus Bullying Prevention Program.

[xxxii] Wood, Wood, Boyd, Wood, Desmarais, 2010.

[xxxiii] Birchmeier, Flaspohler, Elfstrom, Vanderzee, Sink, 2009.

[xxxiv] Pepler and Craig, 2007.

[xxxv] Carney, J. Perceptions of bullying and associated trauma during adolescence. *Professional school counseling, Vol. 11(3).*

[xxxv] World Federation for Mental Health. (2006). World Mental Health Day Project – Building-Awareness-Reducing Risk: Mental Illness and Suicide, Global Education packet. Retrieved from www.wfmh.org on October 10, 2010.

[xxxvi] Your Life Counts. (2010). Bully – 180/Hear from Cindy. Retrieved from www.yourlifecounts.org on October 10, 2010.

[xxxvii] Canadian Mental Health Association. (1993). Signals of Suicide. Retrieved from www.cmha.ca on October 9, 2010.

[xxxviii] World Federation for Mental Health. (2006). World Mental Health Day Project – Building-Awareness-Reducing Risk: Mental Illness and Suicide, Global Education packet. Retrieved from www.wfmh.org on October 10, 2010.

[xxxix] Youth in BC. (2010). *Suicide - Someone I know may be thinking of suicide.* Retrieved from http://youthinbc.com on October 9, 2010.

[xl] Centre for Suicide Prevention. (2007). Communicating with Your Child about Suicide. Retrieved from www.suicideinfo.ca on October 10, 2010.

[xli] Government of Canada – Public Safety. (2005). Long-term

• • •

effects of bullying – children who are victimized. Retrieved from www.publicsafety.gc.ca/res/cp/res/bully-eng September 5, 2011.

[xlii] Dodge, K., Lochman, J. E., Harnish, J. D., Bates, J. E., & Pettit, G. S. (1997). Reactive and proactive aggression in school children and psychiatrically impaired chronically assaultive youth. *Journal of Abnormal Psychology, 106*: 37–51

[xliii] Lewis, D.O., Moy, E., Jackson, L.D., Aaronson, R., Restifo, N., Serra, S., Simos, A. (1985). Biopsychosocial characteristics of children who later murder: A prospective study. *American Journal of Psychiatry, 142*: 1161-1167.

[xliv] Sourander, A., Jensen, P., Ronning, J.A., Elonheimo, H., Niemela, S., Helenius, H. (2007). Childhood bullies and victims and their risk of criminality in late adolescence: The Finnish from a Boy to a Man study. *Archives of Pediatric & Adolescent Medicine, 161*: 546-552.

[xlv] Wasserman G. A., Miller, L.S., and Cothern, L. (2000). *Prevention of Serious and Violent Juvenile Offending.* Washington, D.C.: U.S. Department of Justice

[xlvi] Vossekuil, B., Fein, R., Reddy, M., Borum, R., Modzeleski, W. (2002). *The Final Report and Findings of the Safe School Initiative: Implications for the Prevention of School Attacks in the United States.* Washington: U.S. Department of Education.

[xlvii] Beckman, M. (2004). Crime, culpability, and the adolescent brain. *Science 305*:596–599

[xlviii] Dobb, A.N., Cesaroni, C. (2004). *Responding to Youth Crime in Canada.* Toronto, Ontario, Canada: University of Toronto Press.

[xlix] Christiansen, J. (2009). *Relationship Matters (E-Book).* St. Catharines: Leverage U Press.